Unloved Bull Markets

:d Bull
Markets

*Getting Rich the Easy Way by
Riding Bull Markets*

Craig Callahan

WILEY

For general information on our other products and services or for technical support, please contact our Customer Care Department within the United States at (800) 762-2974, outside the United States at (317) 572-3993 or fax (317) 572-4002.

Wiley also publishes its books in a variety of electronic formats. Some content that appears in print may not be available in electronic formats. For more information about Wiley products, visit our web site at www.wiley.com.

Library of Congress Cataloging-in-Publication Data

Names: Callahan, Craig, author.
Title: Unloved bull markets : getting rich the easy way by riding bull
    markets / Craig Callahan.
Description: Hoboken, New Jersey : Wiley, [2022] | Includes index.
Identifiers: LCCN 2021047306 (print) | LCCN 2021047307 (ebook) | ISBN
    9781119847175 (hardback) | ISBN 9781119847410 (adobe pdf) | ISBN
    9781119847403 (epub)
Subjects: LCSH: Bull markets. | Investments.
Classification: LCC HG4910 .C347 2022 (print) | LCC HG4910 (ebook) | DDC
    332.64/2—dc23/eng/20211004
LC record available at https://lccn.loc.gov/2021047306
LC ebook record available at https://lccn.loc.gov/2021047307

Cover Design: Wiley
Cover Images: © Hryhorii Bondar/Getty Images, © fstop123/Getty Images
SKY10032106_122121

Contents

Preface

This book evolved out of frustration. Many investors, financial advisors, professional money managers, and institutions missed out on the opportunity for big returns and wealth accumulation during the eleven-year bull market from 2009 to 2020 and the subsequent bull market of 2020. We were correctly bullish during those bull markets and were frustrated by our inability to convince audiences that the stock market was going higher. Fears and intuition trumped our data and logic. The investors and managers who missed out were better at denying and dismissing bull markets than they were at recognizing them. The time to rationalize is over. It is time to learn how to recognize a bull market and make money.

For decades I have been telling financial advisors and investors "rallies and bull markets don't issue invitations" and "rallies and bull markets don't look like rallies and bull markets" . . . until they are over. An old Wall Street saying is that "stocks climb a wall of worry." We are in an imperfect world and there is always something to worry about. This book will help financial advisors and investors focus on the profitable climb instead of the worries.

There is a little bit of "I told you so" in this book, but just enough to emphasize a few points and help readers avoid missing the next bull market. Of course, to get the full benefit of the messages in this book, some readers are going to have to admit they were wrong about some things. It seems worth it, though, if that is what it takes to fully participate in the next bull market.

Acknowledgments

I ndeesh Mukhopadhyay provided valuable editorial feedback in the early stages of writing this book. In the final stages, Andrea Weule helped pull it all together. Kevin Scott, director of marketing at ICON, was invaluable with all logistical aspects. I would like to thank all three of them.

When a financial advisor places their investors' assets with ICON, I take it very personally. I would like to thank those advisors for the trust they have placed in me over the years.

I would like to thank my two sons for believing in my system, supporting me, and embracing the duties of being fiduciaries.

I offer special, huge thanks to my wife, Linda, for her love and support, especially during graduate school and the difficult start-up years of ICON.

About the Author

Craig Callahan earned his bachelor of science in psychology at The Ohio State University in 1973 and his doctorate in finance from Kent State University in 1979. He began his career as a finance professor at the University of Denver primarily teaching investments and securities analysis. He also did research for a Denver brokerage firm before cofounding the predecessor company to ICON Advisers in 1986. Dr. Callahan created ICON's valuation investment methodology, which is used by him and others for portfolio management. Since 2000, ICON has won seventeen Lipper Awards for being the number one mutual fund in various categories and time periods. Twice he was a finalist for Ernst & Young's entrepreneur of the year in the Rocky Mountain region. Dr. Callahan appears regularly as a guest on financial television and radio. He does presentations at financial advisor and broker dealer conferences multiple times a year.

Introduction

On March 9, 2009, the stock market hit bottom after a seventeen-month agonizing bear market. Six months earlier, Bear Sterns and Lehman Brothers, two prestigious investment banking firms on Wall Street, collapsed under the weight of subprime mortgages. General Motors was facing bankruptcy and seeking a government bailout. Unemployment was 8.7% and racing to 10%. GDP had been negative for two quarters, including a stunning negative 8.5% quarter-to-quarter drop during the fourth quarter of 2008. Out of that setting, the bull market began. From the low on March 9, 2009, through February19, 2020, the Standard & Poor's (S&P) 1500 Index gained 530.12%, meaning if an investor had the courage to invest $1.00 at the bottom and hold eleven years, $1.00 invested would have grown to $6.30. As impressive as that is, many investors did not participate. Rallies and bull markets are often disguised.

On Monday July 13, 2009, I was on CNBC TV "Squawk on the Street" with Erin Burnett; Matt Nesto, who was substituting for Mark Haines; and another guest, Dan Deighan of Deighan

Financial Advisors. Figure Intro.1 shows the S&P 1500 Index from December 31, 2008, through April 30, 2010. The arrow points at July 13, 2009, the day of the interview. Just prior to the interview the rally took a brief pause late June and early July.

Erin:	How do you position yourself? On the bullish side or the bearish side? Whether you go for a cataclysmic collapse or slow bleed?
Matt (after Mr. Deighan gave his bearish outlook):	Let's get Craig in before he blows a gasket. He's a bull!
Craig:	Yes, I am. It all starts with value. We measure the market right now to be well over 20% below fair value. The corporate bond rally is the best bond rally I have seen in decades and that is very supportive of higher stock prices. Many times we have seen the bond market just pull stocks along with it and I would expect it this time. So we think this is just a pause to the first leg of recovery and we expect the next leg will start soon.
Erin:	And where does that come from? What will be the catalyst for growth?
Craig:	We do not need a robust recovery. We just need the world not to be as terrible as was believed a few months ago. The market did overreact. People were talking depression back then. We are obviously not having one of those, so stocks are just trying to get back to fair value from a time period when people thought we were in a horrible [economic] setting.
Erin:	So you think stocks can go up without any catalyst from where we are now?
Craig (without hesitation):	Yes, we see them going higher.
Erin to Mr. Deighan:	And how low do you see them going? You're saying below the March bottom?
Mr. Deighan:	I see them going below last fall's low as much as 25% to 50% below that.

Erin:	25% to 50% below? Well, that is a great depression scenario.
Mr. Deighan:	That's huge.
Erin:	Where do you see unemployment then?
Mr. Deighan:	I see unemployment getting to 12% to 13%.
Erin:	OK. So, I want a best trade from each of you. Let's start with you Craig.
Craig:	Coach…apparel, purses. The third best performing sector this year has been consumer discretionary. That would surprise many people, but this is an economic anticipation recovery rally and the consumer discretionaries are part of that.
Erin:	And you, Dan?
Dan:	I don't have one. I don't have any buys right now. I think I would sell anything that is based on discretionary spending.

From July 13, 2009, through April 30, 2010, as seen in Figure Intro.1, the S&P 1500 moved higher gaining 35.32% and consumer

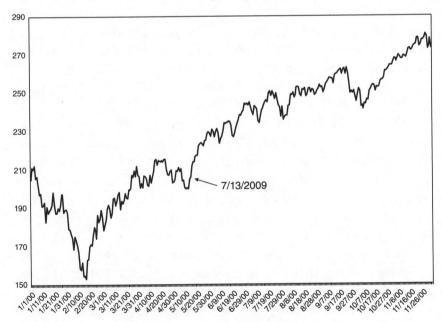

Figure Intro.1   S&P 1500 Index, 12/31/2008–4/30/2010

discretionary was the best sector, gaining 56.98%. Coach was acquired by Tapestry so we can't find a price for it, but Tapestry gained 76.23% over that period. In Chapter 2, we will see that consumer discretionary was the second best performing sector over the eleven-year bull market.

That interview simply shows that one analyst was incorrectly bearish, but the first chapter will offer evidence that many investors did not participate in the bull market, as seen by investors redeeming from equity mutual funds rather than adding to positions to profit from the long-term market advance. Also, as evidence this bull market was "unloved," investor sentiment was much more negative than in the previous two multiyear bull markets.

Those who have missed out try discrediting the bull market stating that it wasn't sensible or was due to gimmicks such as excessively easy monetary policy, bailouts, or corporate buybacks. This book will counter justifications by investors and advisors that this bull market wasn't sensible. The second chapter will show that the long bull market was sensible, had some behaviors and traits similar to previous bull markets, and, therefore, was fairly typical. In the subsequent chapters, the book will examine situations and conditions that bothered investors and could have caused investors to sell or, at least, sit on the sidelines. Looking back, this "wall of worry" was a darn big wall and so was the proportionate climb for stock prices. Let's see if there were lessons to be learned.

The great bull market ended February 19, 2020, just two weeks short of its eleventh birthday. Then the market experienced a twenty-three-trading-day crash, from February 19 to March 23. We could argue that twenty-three days does not qualify as a bear market and that the dip was just an interruption to the multiyear bull market. Because the S&P 1500 Index dropped 34.5% over that period, we would probably lose that argument because a drop of 20% or more is a very popular, although arbitrary, definition of a bear market.

If we concede that the eleven-year bull market ended, then the rally off the March 23, 2020, low must be a new bull market and a spectacular one at that. The NASDAQ Index got back to a new all-time high in fifty-three trading days. The S&P 500 Index took

103 trading days. If the eleven-year bull market was "unloved," its sequel was downright despised, as shown by the bearish, skeptical, negative commentary that dominated print and broadcast media.

As in 2009, I was interviewed just before and after the bottom and provided a bullish outlook. In an interview with nationally syndicated financial columnist Chuck Jaffe that aired on his podcast "Money Life" on March 20, 2020, one trading day before the bottom, I stated, "Best bargains we have ever seen." Mr. Jaffe then asked, "When do you buy?" I responded, "There are all of the supportive conditions typical of buying opportunities. I think that it is a matter of days or weeks. We're close." A week and a half later, on CNBC TV "The Exchange," I declared, "We do believe a bottom is forming and it seems like all the bad news is priced in."

The two recent bull markets that began March 2009 and March 2020 seemed obvious to us but not to most investors.

Chapter 1
"Unloved" Bull Markets

Along with many other observers, Tom Keene of Bloomberg Surveillance Radio called the multiyear bull market, from March 2009 to February 2020, "unloved." We agree and believe that, for a variety of reasons, many investors chose not to participate in the market and missed out on a terrific opportunity to increase wealth. In previous bull markets, investors gained confidence and faith as the market advanced. Not this one. Unlike in previous bull markets, investors neither gained confidence nor faith in the workings of the market. If anything, the advance only encouraged the opposite: skepticism and doubt.

The Investment Company Institute (ICI) reports mutual fund data in its annual Investment Company Fact Book regarding annual inflows, outflows, and net flows for equity mutual funds beginning in 1984. Figure 1.1 shows annual net flows, which is inflows (sales) minus outflows (redemptions) in millions of dollars in gray scaled on the right. The S&P 500 Index is in black with quarterly observations scaled on the left.

Although the bull market in the early 1980s began in August 1982, equity fund flow data begin in 1984. Nevertheless, we see increasing positive flows in 1984, 1985, 1986, and 1987 as the S&P 500 moved higher. The market advance attracted investors, as they apparently gained confidence. There were net outflows in

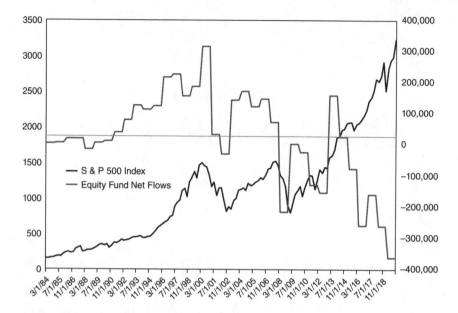

Figure 1.1   Equity Fund Net Flows and S&P 500 Index, 1984–2019

1988 as investors moved away from equities after the market crash of October 1987. As it happens investors were captivated by the crash in their rearview mirrors and couldn't bear to face the bull market ahead.

As the next bull market started, equity mutual fund net flows turned positive and grew accordingly with the market advance. The graph shows how the rising market enticed investors to buy equity mutual funds. In the end of that bull market, net flows hit their peak concurrent with the high of the S&P 500 Index. During the market decline following the "tech bubble" of early 2000, investors greatly reduced their investing into equity mutual funds. As the market advanced off the September 2002 low, investors sent net positive flows into equity mutual funds, not to the extent seen in the late 1990s but still enough to reflect confidence and optimism for equities.

Compared to the previous bull markets post 1987 and 2002, what makes this recent bull market "unloved"? The surge off the market low in early 2009 barely got net flows positive, but 2010, 2011, and 2012 saw a race for the exits even though the market moved higher. Unable to see the multiyear bull market ahead of them, the only emotions investors were capable of was simply, "Get me out of here!" Only one year, 2013, saw significant net positive flows, but after that brief period of confidence in equities, investors reverted to a negative view, especially in 2016, 2017, and 2018. These net redemptions were clearly early as the S&P 500 hit an all-time high February 2020 and those who redeemed along the way did not participate.

Outflows continued as the market moved higher in 2019, as reported in the *Wall Street Journal* December 9, 2019, in a front page article with the title "Individual Investors Bail on Stocks." "The S&P 500 is having its best run in six years, but individual investors are fleeing stock funds at the fastest pace in decades." It continued, "Investors have pulled $135.5 billion from U.S. stock-focused mutual funds and exchange traded funds so far this year, the biggest withdrawals on record, according to data provider Refinitiv Lipper, which tracked the data going back to 1992."

Table 1.1 shows the average annual net flows into equity mutual funds for four bull markets. It was positive for the previous three bull markets but negative for the most recent one. The market was moving higher but investors were fleeing equities, unusual, but explained by investor sentiment in the next section.

Table 1.1 Average Annual Net Flows (in $ Millions)

1984–1987	12,649
1988–1999	106,520
2003–2007	132,040
2009–2019	–112,279

Investor Sentiment

The America Association of Individual Investors (AAII) conducts a weekly investment sentiment survey of its members. It asks, "Are you bullish, neutral, or bearish?," meaning, does the respondent think the stock market is going higher, sideways, or lower? The survey began July 1987. Figure 1.2 shows a rolling four-week average of the percent bullish divided by the percent bearish from July 1987 through February 2020. The middle line is the average for the entire time period, right near 1.50%, meaning typically three bulls for every two bears. The other two lines are one standard deviation above and below average. Before focusing on the recent bull market, some general observations are noteworthy. This group can really be wrong sometimes. The two arrows above highlight some extremes like the excessive bullishness precrash 1987 and at the tech bubble peak of early 2000. Those were terrible times to be bullish. The four

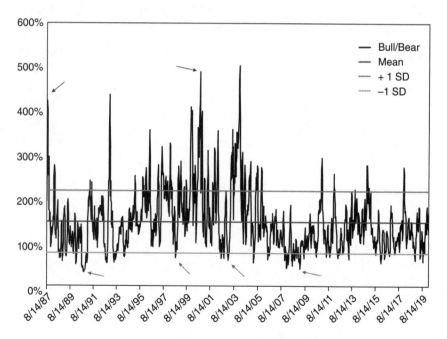

Figure 1.2   AAII Bull/Bear Ratio, Four-Week Average

arrows at the bottom represent great buying opportunities when the market went higher but investors were extremely (incorrectly) bearish: 1990, 1998, 2003, and 2009.

For the eleven-year bull market from 2009 through 2020, the bull/bear ratio is generally below average. There are a few quick bursts of optimism, when the bull/bear ratio got one standard deviation above the long-term average, but the optimism is nowhere near the magnitude or duration of those that occurred in previous bull markets. This group was mostly wrong the entire way up, frequently posting bull/bear ratios one standard deviation below the historic average.

Table 1.2 shows the average bull/bear reading during four bull markets based on the weeks when the bull market began and ended. Perhaps the bull market of December 1987 through February 1994 was "unloved" also because its average bull/bear ratio was similarly low as the recent bull market. In Chapter 2 we make the case that the sharp market drop in October 2008 was a "crash" and similar to the crash of October 1987. Perhaps severe sudden drops in the market affect investors' sentiment for the subsequent bull market. Maybe crashes inflict some psychological damage. In any case, investors were much more bullish during the bull markets of the late 1990s and early 2000s. In summary, during this recent bull market, investors usually, and incorrectly, thought the market was going to go lower. We can only presume that they did not fully participate in the bountiful returns. That would seem to qualify as "unloved."

As evidence that the bull market was "unloved" we saw investors pulling money from equity mutual funds unlike during previous

Table 1.2 Average Weekly Bull/Bear Ratio (in %)

12/1987–2/1994	125.0
12/1994–3/2000	188.3
9/2002–10/2007	174.5
3/2009–2/2020	126.3

bull markets. Investor sentiment explained that behavior because investors had a more negative view of the market than in the previous two bull markets. This doubt and skepticism were not limited to the individual investor. Some institutional investors, acting as fiduciaries and often presumed to be more sophisticated, demonstrated the same lack of love for equities.

Public Funds Pension Plans and Endowments

Public Funds are pension plans for state and local governments and professionals like firefighters and police. Employees are elected to a board that manages the plan, usually with the advice of a pension consultant. Public Funds Data, a website, provides data on more than six thousand of these plans nationwide. Figure 1.3 shows equities as a percent of assets for those plans from 2001 through 2020. During the bull market from 2003 to 2007 the plans held about 60%

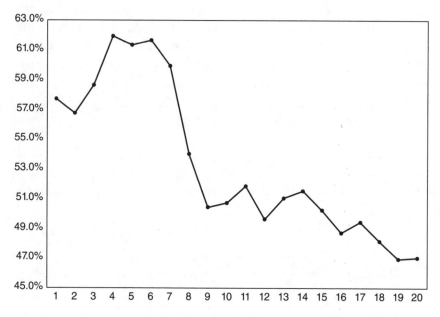

Figure 1.3   Public Funds, Equities as a Percent of Assets

of their assets in equities, but after the bear market of 2008, the percentage dropped to near 50% and gradually drifted lower as the stock market moved higher. By tracking equity asset percentage, we can measure the confidence institutional investors had in the market. If they had believed in a continuing strong stock market, they could have increased the equity exposure back up to 60%, but they did not. In fact, equity exposure trended lower during the eleven-year bull market.

It appears the decreased equity exposure cost the pension plans returns for the benefit of their constituents. As public funds diversify among asset classes that historically have underperformed equities, such as bonds, some alternatives, and some real estate, it is normal for them to lag an all-equity index during a bull market. From 2003 through 2007, average annual return of public funds was 9.78%, lagging the S&P 500, which averaged 13.15% per year. From 2009 through 2019, the amount of lag expanded, probably due to the reduction of equity exposure. Plan annual return was only 4.47% versus the S&P 500 Index of 15.26%.

Barron's covered institutional low-equity exposure in "The Case for Stocks," by Andrew Bary, July 22, 2019. "Many big public pension funds like Calpers and endowments, which have big investments in alternative assets such as private equity and hedge funds, failed to beat the S&P 500 or even a 75%/25% mix of stocks and bonds the decade that ended June 2018. The Yale endowment, led by David Swensen, has just 3% of its portfolio in U.S. stocks and as a result has failed to participate fully in the huge market gains of the past ten years."

An article by Barry Ritholtz on *Bloomberg News,* October 9, 2019, titled "Ivy League Endowments Make the Same Old Mistakes," stated,

> The latest university endowment return data dribbling out for the fiscal year ended June 30 is not pretty. Harvard's endowment gained 6.5%; while Yale's had an increase of just 5.7%; the University of Pennsylvania endowment gained 6.5%; Dartmouth yielded 7.5%. During the same time period, investors in the Standard & Poor's 500 Index had total returns, which includes dividends, of

10.4%; a portfolio of 60% stocks and 40% bonds returned 9.9%. This performance is consistent with the record of the past decade, with none of the Ivy endowments beating a 60–40 portfolio in the 2008–2018 period, though a couple did come close.

The article then continues, "The biggest contributors to the weak performance of the endowments were high exposure to hedge funds (2019 returns = 1.1%) and natural resources (2019 returns= −6.8%)."

An article in *Barron's,* October 14, 2019, with the title "Bull Market Beats Yale," stated in its tag line, "U.S. university endowments, heavy in alternatives, again underperform stocks and bonds. Time for a change in the model." The author, Nicholas Jasinski then pointed out, "The S&P 500 has produced annualized returns of 14.7% in that [ten-year] span, and a stock/bond mix has posted 11.4% gains a year—but the average return of 149 colleges and universities analyzed by Cambridge Associates was 8.6%."

The eleven-year bull market had so much to offer, yet individual investors and institutional investors alike didn't fully participate. Occasionally articles appear talking about public funds being underfunded relative to their future pension obligations. It seems the first place to look is their asset allocation decision and reduced exposure to stocks. As for college endowments, perhaps it is easier to ask alumni for more money than it is to recognize and participate in a bull market.

For both public funds and endowments their use of "alternatives" is puzzling. One feature of alternatives, like some hedge funds, is their attempt to be low in correlation with the stock market. Low correlation is a diversification tool to reduce overall portfolio volatility, but why should public funds and endowments care about volatility? It would seem that they have an investment time horizon of twenty to thirty years. We have argued, in an article coauthored with Tom Howard, that volatility is not the correct definition of risk. We suggested underperforming an investor's retirement goal is risk. With the growth of alternative investments, we have often asked the question, "Who needs an alternative to making 530% in eleven years?"

Anecdotal Examples of Unloved

Investors or reporters would often ask, "Why did the stock market go up today?" Their tone clearly conveyed skepticism and the belief that the stock market should not be going higher. The simple, correct, but flippant answer would have been, "We are in a bull market, stock prices are supposed to go higher!" That answer would not have worked because people do not like being told they are wrong, and they did not realize a bull market was under way.

Even the terminology used to describe the market conveyed the unloved nature. The short-term dips of 5% to 10% were called *corrections*, which implied that the market was not supposed to be going higher and that it was correcting itself by going down. As we know now, the correct path was upward. The market was supposed to be going higher. In our research department, just to keep our sanity and our long-term view intact, we labeled those dips *incorrections*.

In previous bull markets, if the market was higher one day, there would be more buying the next day by momentum investors. It is often referred to as "fear of missing the boat" as it is pulling away from the dock. In a bull market it is usually a terrible feeling seeing the market move higher while holding cash. During this bull market, however, if the market was higher on a day the next day saw a sell-off thirty to sixty minutes into the trading day. It felt like investors, not realizing we were in a bull market, felt the advance the day before gave them a chance to get out. So to move higher two days in a row, buyers had to take out the weak jittery money.

One metric used by investors who use technical analysis is comparing the number of issues that advance each day to the number that decline. If over a recent period of, say, ten or thirty days a lot more issues are advancing than declining, there are two interpretations. One is that the advance has breadth and is sustainable. The other is that the market is "overbought" and will soon turn and go lower. Commentary during the bull market typically favored the negative view as the market was labeled "overbought." It appears that the analyst's predetermined bearish bias influenced the interpretation of the data.

For the eleven-year bull market and especially for the new one that began March 2020, there is a new generation of investor. These new investors are very situational. They don't believe in the broad market, just special situations like the unique stories of Amazon or Tesla. In the early stages of the 2020 bull market, it was the "work from home" theme. How would investors behave if they didn't believe in the bull market but just invested or speculated in a stock they think is unique? They tend to be jittery and set very quick sell thresholds that we believe explains some of the volatility and rapid theme changes that occurred during the eleven-year bull market and the new 2020 bull market.

Confidence

Every week *Barron's* computes and publishes its Confidence Index. The editors define it as the ratio of the yield on high-grade bonds divided by the yield on intermediate-grade bonds. Think of it as measuring the confidence investors have in the financial system. Naturally investors need a higher yield on the riskier intermediate-grade bonds than they do on the higher rated bonds. If the two yields are very close, say high-grade is 95% of intermediate-grade, investors have confidence in the system and the ability of intermediate-grade companies to honor their payments. But if there is a wide yield gap, say the yield on higher-grade bonds is only 60% of the much higher yield on intermediate-grade bonds, investors would be showing little confidence in the financial system and intermediate-grade companies' abilities to honor their payments.

Figure 1.4 shows the Confidence Index from December 29, 1978, through February 21, 2020. The straight line represents the average reading for three different time periods. It averaged 93.2 from December 29, 1978, through December 31, 1999. Then it dropped and averaged 83.5 from January 7, 2000, through December 31, 2008. From January 2, 2009, through February 21, 2020, covering the eleven-year bull market and a couple of months before it began, it averaged only 73.5. This recent bull market took place in a setting of low investor confidence in the financial system.

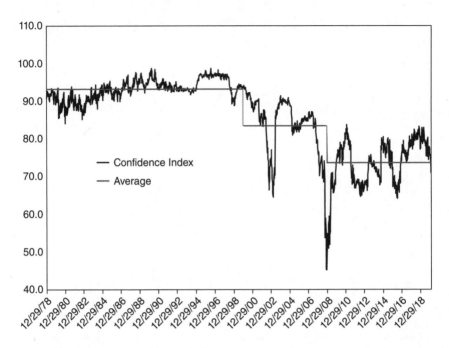

Figure 1.4 Barron's Confidence Index, 12/29/1978–2/21/2020

We contend an investor's confidence affects how he or she receives and processes news. If confidence is high, bad news might get dismissed or softened in its perception. If confidence is low, bad news is on the fast track to negative sensors. During this bull market, investors were viewing the glass as half empty. In this state, they were overly sensitive to mediocre and bad news, with good news or bullish indicators flying under their radar. It is almost as if they were screaming, "Don't tell me facts, I'm too scared to listen."

Yields Suggest "Unloved"

Interest payments on 10-year Treasury notes are fixed over the life of the note. Dividends for companies in the S&P 500 Index have grown through the years. As seen in Figure 1.5 of year-end yields for the 10-year Treasury and the S&P 500 Index, the yield

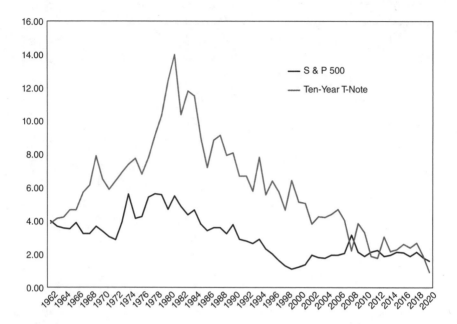

Figure 1.5   Yields: S&P 500 and 10-Year Treasury 1962–2020

is usually higher for the 10-year Treasury. Investors are willing to accept a lower current yield on stocks because they expect the dividends to grow. Since 1962, the yield on the 10-year Treasury has exceeded the yield on the S&P 500, on average, by about 300 basis points.

There have been six times when the yield on the S&P 500 Index has been greater than the yield on the 10-year Treasury: year-ends 1962, 2008, 2011, 2012, 2019, and 2020. Once the two were about equal: year-end 2015. What was going on these seven times to reverse a normal, rational yield relationship? News events at the time of a few of these could explain investor behavior. The Cuban Missile Crisis was October 1962. The financial crisis was October 2008. The European debt crisis round two was September 2011. Investors were obviously afraid of owning stocks and were clinging to the safety of Treasury notes. They sold stocks and bid up the price of the Treasury notes, which lowered their yield. Five times during this multiyear bull market, investors disliked stocks so much, we were offered a higher yield on the S&P 500 than on the 10-year Treasury, despite the potential for the S&P 500 to provide dividend growth and capital appreciation. We had not seen this desperate yield relationship for forty-six years, then it appeared five times just before and during this multiyear bull market.

When the yield on the S&P 500 is equal to or exceeding the yield on the 10-year Treasury it signals that stocks are cheap and bonds are expensive. It is telling us investors like bonds and dislike equities and has been a very good "buy" signal for equities. Table 1.3 shows the rates of return for the S&P 500 for one and two years after the seven times of unusual relative yields.

Table 1.3   Rates of Return for the S&P 500 (%)

Year	One-Year	Two-Year
1962	22.8	42.9
2008	26.5	45.5
2011	16.0	53.6
2012	34.6	53.0
2015	12.0	36.4
2019	18.3	???
2020	???	???

Other Assets

It might have been alright to miss out on the bull market in domestic equities if similar returns could have been earned in other types of assets, but that is not the case. Domestic equities were clearly the sweet spot of investing during the multiyear bull market. Figure 1.6 shows cumulative returns for 2009 through 2019 for the S&P 1500 Index, Gold, the Commodities Research Board (CRB) Index, three bond indexes, and the Consumer Price Index. Although the nonstock assets beat inflation, they trailed equities severely. The stock market was the place to be and missing out on the bull market was a big deal.

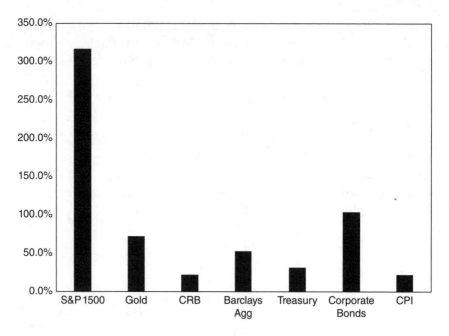

Figure 1.6   Cumulative Return 2009–2019

Does Rate of Return Matter?

You bet it does. From the low on March 9, 2009, to the peak on February 19, 2020, the S&P 500 Index gained at an annual rate of 18.3%. We will not use that for this example because it was above average and exceptional. Let's tone it down and use 10% per year, right near the historic average for equities. Figure 1.7 shows the growth of $1.00 over twenty years at 10% per year. It also shows the growth at 5% per year, a rate slightly above what the public fund pension plans earned during the bull market.

Of course, for the public funds the starting amount could easily be $1 billion, so after twenty years there is a $4 billion gap for each billion invested. Even after ten years the gap is almost $1 billion per billion invested. For an individual investor, if the starting amount is $100,000 the difference is over a $400,000 after twenty years. The same math applies to financial advisors for whom the primary determinant of the value of their practice is assets under management.

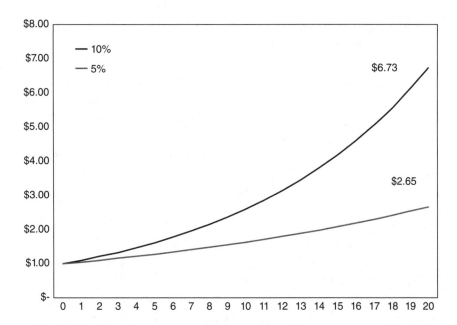

Figure 1.7 Compounding at 10% and 5%

The higher returns earned by the investors, the more the value of the practice grows. Rate of return and participating in bull markets matter because if the goal for retirement is to buy a residence in a tropical location or to travel, the seller of the residence or the travel agent doesn't take risk-adjusted returns. They take money. If the investor can tolerate a little volatility, the market can do the heavy lifting to get to retirement goals.

A couple of years before the end of the eleven-year bull market, I was working out at my fitness center in Naples, Florida. A stock market channel was on most of the TVs and the market was up that day. One retired fellow joked to his buddies, "If the stock market keeps going up, I'll actually be able to afford my life style."

Top Ten Reasons I Missed the Bull Market

Throughout this multiyear bull market we wrote papers addressing concerns such as unemployment, inflation, deflation, double-dip recession, rising interest rates and monetary policy, and so on that were keeping investors from being invested. These conditions will be addressed in more depth in later chapters. Our presentations were logical and full of data and statistics, but we suspect not successful in getting investors to overcome their fears. In 2015, we tried a different approach and poked fun at investors who were missing out on the bull market. We borrowed from David Letterman and his top-ten lists that he used on his "Late Night Show." We could not limit the list to ten, so we called it "The Top 15 Reasons I Missed the Bull Market." Here they are as written in 2015:

15. I didn't notice S&P 500 earnings have grown 107% from 2008.
14. After 2008, I changed my risk tolerance.
13. I am stuck in the 1970s and thought inflation would come back and interest rates would rise.
12. I was waiting for unemployment to get below 5%.
11. I bought gold instead of equities.
10. I didn't like the bailouts.
9. I don't understand the Federal Reserve and thought the government was "printing money."
8. I forgot every economic recovery is different and I was waiting for housing to recover.
7. I heard Fed easing was like "pushing on a string."
6. I saw a head and shoulders top-forming a few times.
5. I thought P/E ratios were too high.
4. I was told we are in a seventeen-year secular bear market.
3. I worried about deflation and Greek sovereign debt.
2. My accountant told me I didn't need huge capital gains.

And the number one reason I missed the bull market of the last six years is:

1. I really like earning nothing on CDs.
Some of these will be addressed in later chapters. Thanks, David!

Unloved? Why?

Figure 1.8 is the S&P 1500 Index from January 30, 2009 (about one month before the bottom) through the peak February 2020. Impressive, as even a cursory look boggles the mind. There were a few dips and pauses along the way but with 20/20 hindsight it appears it would have been easy to just buy and hold and go for the profitable ride. So why did investors net redeem out of equity mutual funds? Why was investor sentiment mostly below average? Why did public funds reduce their equity exposure as a percent of assets? What was happening that kept investors from embracing this bull market like they did previous bull markets?

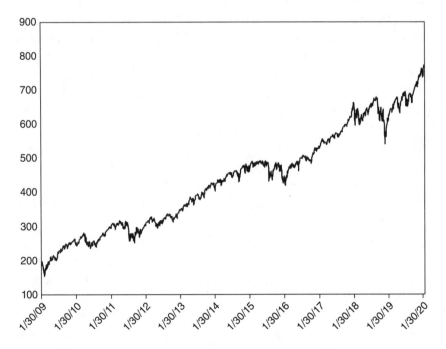

Figure 1.8 S&P 1500 Index 1/30/09–2/19/20

Throughout the eleven years there was no shortage of skeptical, bearish commentary in the financial media and from advisory services and professional money managers. As for the books, one of the early ones, first published in 2010 and updated in 2012, predicted a decade of slow economic growth and deflation based on deleveraging. Regarding stocks, the author predicted falling P/E ratios, muted price appreciation, and recommended avoiding stocks related to big ticket consumer purchases, consumer lending, and homebuilding. He favored buying Treasury bonds, consumer staples, and North American energy. (Chapter 2 will confirm how wrong these predictions and recommendations were.) A second book in 2014 based its view on demographics and predicted the economy would fall off a cliff and that the stock market would be terrible from 2014 to 2019. The author warned that you needed to prepare for the worst downturn and crash of your lifetime beginning in early to mid-2014. A third book in 2018 labeled the bull market "fake" and claimed we could fake a bull market for just a short, limited amount of time. The author based the potential for a severe market reversal on global debt and Federal Reserve policy. Rather than fake, a 530% gain in eleven years and a 765% gain through August 2021 seems very real to an investor who participated. Did the books influence investors and contribute to their bearish sentiment or did investors' predetermined bearish position simply make them receptive the gloom and doom theme? Maybe a little of both.

As for regular commentary, there were fears of higher inflation, deflation, double-dip recession, and rising interest rates at various times along the way. Early on many skeptics didn't like what they called "bailouts." Some thought the easy monetary policy made the bull market phony, fabricated, and unsustainable. Some investors did not think the unemployment rate was dropping fast enough. Negative interest rates, new and puzzling for this generation, scared many investors away. Valuation seemed to be a problem for many because there were frequent claims that stocks were too expensive. Chapter by chapter, let's look into these situations and see if there was a lesson to be learned. After all, there will be more bull markets in the future, and we don't want to miss out on them.

Chapter 2
Was the Bull Market Sensible?

W e can only assume that investors and money managers
with bearish sentiments sitting in cash must have been
baffled by the market advances. By no measure could
the bull market have been considered sensible to these doubters,
because it behaved against all of their expectations. Was it unusual?
Actually not. This chapter will show that it was very typical regarding annual returns, sector returns, and in rewarding volatility tolerance. It was sensible based on fundamentals such as earnings and
value. Even its daily behavior in terms of up days and down days
was typical of bull markets, and it had the usual big day surges.

Annual Returns

Originally assembled by Ibbotson & Associates, we have data on the
S&P 500 Index back to 1926. Figure 2.1 shows annual returns in a
frequency distribution. For example, twenty-one years the return was
between 10% and 20% (tall column in the middle). The annual return
is positive 74% of the years. Returns are fairly normally distributed
(bell-shaped curve) with a slight skew. The average annual return has
been 12.4%, and the compounded annual return has been 10.6%.

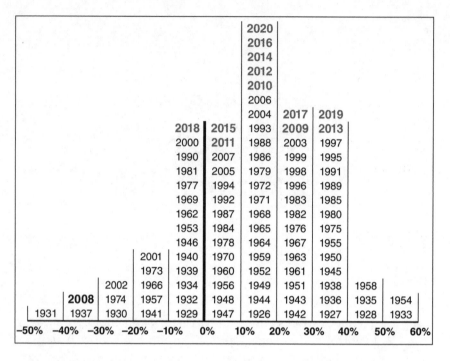

Figure 2.1 S&P 500 Annual Returns (1926–2020)

Before looking at the returns during the bull market, 2008 stands out as a very unusual year with its negative 37% return being second lowest out of ninety-five years. The twelve years since 2008 are very normal with five being the most frequently seen return of +10% to +20%, two each in the 0% to 10% and 20% to 30%, one in the −10% to 0%, and two in the 30% to 40% ranges. It appears that during the last twelve years the stock market was just being the stock market, doing what it has done for ninety-five years.

Sectors and Volatility

Table 2.1 shows the rates of returns from the market low March 9, 2009, through the then all-time high February 19, 2020. Over this time period, the S&P 1500 Index gained 530.1%, meaning $1.00 invested

Table 2.1 Rates of Return from the Market Low, 3/9/2009–2/19/2020

Sector	S&P 1500 Sector Index Return: 3/9/09 through 2/19/20 (%)	Average Beta vs. S&P 1500 Index (stocks within ICON database)
Information Technology	932.9	1.16
Consumer Discretionary	839.5	1.02
Financials	625.8	1.09
Industrials	584.5	1.15
S&P 1500 Index	530.1	1.00
Health Care	520.0	1.01
Real Estate	482.7	0.81
Utilities	395.6	0.66
Materials	365.3	1.15
Consumer Staples	359.4	0.85
Telecommunication Services	261.9	0.90
Energy	67.9	1.26

at the low would be worth $6.30 on February 19, 2020. Impressive, but far behind the 932.9% return on the S&P 1500 Information Technology Index over the same time period, meaning $1.00 invested in that index at the bottom would have grown to $10.32. Three other S&P 1500 sector indexes beat the broad market: the S&P 1500 Consumer Discretionary Index, up 839.5%; the S&P 1500 Financials Index, up 625.8%; and the S&P 1500 Industrials Index, up 584.5%.

What ought to stand out immediately is that the leaders were either cyclical or economically sensitive, and some of the laggards were the defensive, so-called recession-proof sectors: telecommunication services, utilities, and consumer staples. The returns in the table suggest that a rewarding strategy during this eleven-year run was to believe in, and invest in, the economic recovery and expansion through sectors like consumer discretionary, information technology, and industrials. Looking back, one of the most frequently touted concerns during this period was that the consumer would stop shopping and buying, a concern that, based on the performance of the consumer discretionary sector, appears misguided. In addition, it appears believing that financials would right the ship and recover from the financial crisis of 2008 was rewarded. At the other end, investors who doubted the recovery and expansion and preferred defensive sectors would have missed out on higher returns.

Before addressing the right column, a little background on beta can be useful. It was introduced by William Sharpe in the 1960s as a measure of volatility. A stock with a beta greater than 1.00 is more volatile than the broad market and a stock with a beta less than 1.00 is less volatile than the market. When first introduced, scholars suggested it made managing money easy because managers should simply hold high beta stocks in bull (rising) markets and low beta stocks in bear (declining) markets. A portfolio correctly following this practice would beat indexes during both bull markets (going up more) and bear markets (going down less). This sounds good in theory. A problem, however, as we have seen with the eleven-year bull market, is that mangers are not good at knowing whether they are in a bull or bear market.

The right column in the table is the average beta for the stocks in each sector in the ICON database versus the S&P 1500 Index. As for the eleven-year bull market, the table shows that the top five performing sectors have average betas greater than 1.00 and, generally, the sectors with low betas lagged. So the scholars' textbook recommendation was in effect as it was rewarding to hold high beta stocks in a bull market. (As exceptions, energy and materials were two high-beta sectors that lagged, but we believe these sectors have added volatility and higher betas because of commodity price influences.)

Buying and holding these leading sectors was not easy. During market declines the cyclical, economically sensitive sectors dropped more than the market, and the defensive, recession-proof sectors held up better. These were complete reversals of the long-term theme. Table 2.2 shows how sectors ranked during the sharp declines of 2010, 2011, and 2018, the three most severe setbacks during the bull market. The first two were the European debt crisis rounds one and two when the S&P 1500 dropped 15.8% and 19.4%,

Table 2.2 Sector Ranked During Market Declines in 2010, 2011, and 2018

Sector	4/23/10– 7/2/10 Rank	7/7/11–10/3/11 Rank	9/20/18–12/24/18 Rank	Average
Communication Services	1	3	5	3.0
Utilities	2	1	1	1.3
Consumer Staples	3	2	3	2.7
Health Care	4	5	4	4.3
Real Estate	5	7	2	4.7
Information Technology	6	4	9	6.3
Industrials	7	9	10	8.7
Consumer Discretionary	8	6	7	7.0
Financials	9	10	6	8.3
Materials	10	11	8	9.7
Energy	11	8	11	10.0

respectively. During the sharp drop of 19.8% in 2018, investors worried about the Federal Reserve potentially tightening monetary policy in 2019. We have labeled all three "volatility events" and discuss them in more detail in Chapter 9. In all three cases, long-term leaders like consumer discretionary, information technology, financials, and industrials ranked an average of 6.3 or worse, which means they dropped more than average. Sticking with those long-term leaders would have taken fortitude and long-term vision.

To summarize sector and volatility behavior in the eleven-year bull market, investors were rewarded for seeking and tolerating volatility by buying and holding high-beta stocks in economically sensitive, cyclical sectors. To get the full benefit of the eleven-year bull market they had to ride through some severe reversals. To that extent, it was a fairly normal, classic bull market. Investors who believed in the economy and tolerated volatility got rewarded. Textbook bull market.

Earnings

Was the bull market sensible from a corporate earnings perspective? In other words, did earnings grow and support higher valuations? Figure 2.2 shows earnings per share for the S&P 1500 Index, which includes companies in the S&P 500 (large-cap), S&P Mid-Cap 400, and the S&P Small-Cap 600. It shows the drop in earnings for 2008 and 2009 during the recession. Although some banks posted losses, overall, the 1500 companies had positive earnings in 2008 and 2009, just lower than in 2006 and 2007. Although there was growth during the eleven-year bull market, there was a pause in 2015 and 2016, a result of the drop in the price of oil and the gains in the value of the US dollar. As of this writing, 2021, 2022, and 2023 shown in the graph are estimates from a survey of analysts. From 2009 through 2019, coinciding with the bull market, earnings grew at a compounded annual rate of 9.9% per year. Earnings in the best

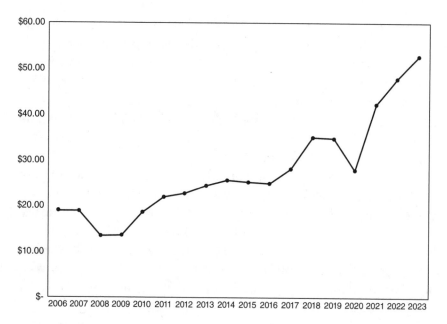

Figure 2.2   S&P 1500 Earnings Per Share 2006–2023

two performing sectors, information technology and consumer discretionary, grew at 14.3% and 13.8% per year, respectively. Based on earnings, the bull market appears sensible. Although some investors worried about various uncertainties at the macroeconomic level, companies went about their business of growing profits, and stock prices responded.

Value

At ICON, we compute intrinsic value for stocks. We never use simplistic ratios like price/earnings (P/E) or price-to-book value. To compute value, we take average earnings and project earnings growing out into the future at growth rates forecasted by analysts. Then we discount those future earnings back to their present value considering risk and interest rates. Fundamentally it is very similar to the theory of the dividend discount model, just building off of earnings rather than dividends. The equation is applied to approximately 1,700 domestic stocks. Value is divided by price for a value/price (V/P) ratio.

Figure 2.3 shows the S&P 1500 Index in gray from February 1, 2009, just before the market bottom in early March, the then-all-time high in February 2020. The black line is ICON's estimate of fair value based on the average V/P ratio of the 1700 stocks.

What stands out is that prices grew but fair value also grew. In other words, fair value was an upwardly moving target for prices. Prices just tried to keep up with value.

This figure illustrates the very foundation of a "value" manager's view of the stock market. As earnings grow, value grows, and prices just try to keep up. When the news is good, investors get optimistic and prices get ahead of value. When the news is bad, investors get concerned and prices lag behind value. Price tries to keep up with value. News and emotions just get in the way sometimes.

There is a big gap between value and price during both of the European Debt Crises in 2010 and 2011 when investors worried that potential sovereign debt defaults would cause a recession. From this

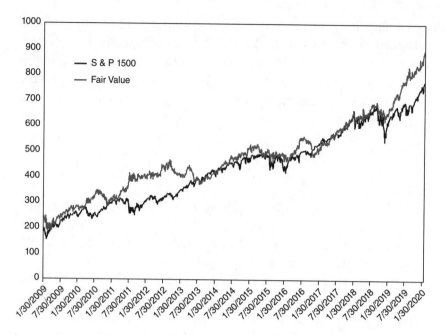

Figure 2.3   S&P 1500 Index and Fair Value

perspective those two rapid sell-offs appear very irrational and fear based, an overreaction to economic conditions. Also noteworthy is how close value and price were during the second half of this bull market. Other than a couple of times when price and value were 10% to 15% apart (pre-election 2016 and December 2018) we don't see extreme optimism reflected in overpricing nor the extreme fear that accompanies underpricing. Overall, based on value, the great bull market of 2009–2020 was rational and sensible. During that bull market we were frequently in disagreement with analysts who incorrectly thought stocks were expensive.

Down Days

Naturally, in multiyear bull markets the market does not go up every day. There are down days for a variety of reasons such as profit taking, negative news, or some economic data released that fall short of estimates. When the market experiences a down day it can be frustrating to those invested who believe the market should be advancing. Just the opposite, down days can serve as confirmation to those on the sidelines holding cash. Let's compare multiyear bull markets to see their "down-day" behavior.

Since 1982 we have identified five multiyear bull markets; 8/82–8/87, 12/87–2/94, 12/94–3/00, 9/02–10/07, and the recent one 3/09–2/20. We chose to split the advance from 1987 to 2000 into two bull markets because there was a sideways move in 1994. The S&P 1500 came into existence 1/1/1995 so the last two bull markets use it for counting days and the earlier two markets use the S&P 500. For the 12/94 to 3/2000 bull market, we used mostly the 1500 Index but patched in the 500 for the one month of 1994.

Table 2.3 shows the total number of days from the bottom to the top and how many days the market dropped. As a percentage, all five bull markets are pretty similar in terms of percent of days that the market goes down, generally between 44% and 46%. The recent bull market appears quite average at 44.8%. In fact, it is right in the middle. Based on the percentage of down days, there is no reason for this bull market to have been unloved. It was actually pretty typical.

Notice what the percentage of down days means for a bullish investor who has correctly assessed that we are in a bull market and is in a buy-and-hold mode. Almost half the time the market goes

Table 2.3 Bull Markets

Dates	Total Days	Down Days	% Down Days	% Total Return	% Best Days
8/1982–8/1987	1274	589	46.2	304	5.1
12/1987–2/1994	1559	723	46.4	163	2.7
12/1994–3/2000	1335	595	44.6	261	4.2
9/2002–10/2007	1258	557	44.3	125	2.7
3/2009–2/2020	2758	1236	44.8	530	2.3

against that position. Buying and holding, the correct posture in a multiyear bull market, takes some fortitude and discipline when the market goes down almost half the days. Now, for the investor with the incorrect view that the market is in a bear market and is on the sidelines holding cash, he or she gets confirmation that the incorrect view is correct 2 to 2.5 days per week on average. ICON put out a paper entitled "Rallies Don't Look Like Rallies!" in late 2009 pointing this out to investors. In other words, rallies don't go straight up like an investor may want. It was an attempt to get investors to overlook the down days and get invested for the long term.

How can you gain 530% in eleven years if the market goes down almost half the time? Well, there are some really big up (surge) days. What if an investor could only be invested on the really good, best days? Impossible we believe, but it is worth computing to illustrate the personality of multiyear bull markets. We ranked the days from best to worst and then went down the list, compounding daily returns. The column on the far right shows what percentage of the total days an investor would need to be invested to obtain the return of the entire bull market. For example, in the recent bull market, if an investor could have been in the very best days, it would have meant being invested in just 2.3% of the 2,758 days to earn 530%.

This recent bull market has been typical of multiyear bull markets in that a large part of the total return was concentrated in the large surge days. The fact that this recent bull market is in the low end in terms of best days required suggests it has experienced more big surge days than normal for a bull market, which may have contributed to some observations. Momentum investors did not excel during this eleven-year advance. Perhaps by the time their momentum-driven buy threshold was registered, the big gains were already recorded. The active management versus passive (indexing) investing will be covered later, but the surge nature of this bull market may have hurt active managers. If cash came into a mutual fund and was not immediately invested it could have missed important big days. Finally, you may have heard the phrase "risk on, risk off," which we believe is a synonym for short-term market timing. Similar to the momentum investors, investors practicing this approach may have missed big days and spotted the market a head start during short-term advances. We believe the buy-and-hold approach beat the timers because it was likely to participate in the big days.

Similar Crashes, Similar Recoveries

The "crash" of October 1987 happened in a day. In October 2008, the market dropped a similar amount but over the course of a week. It wasn't labeled a crash, but if you graph the S&P 500 Index on a weekly basis the drops are almost duplicates. The market actions immediately after those two events were different because there actually was a recession following the 2008 crash, whereas the recession feared in late 1987 never occurred. Nevertheless, the long-term market recoveries were remarkably similar.

Figure 2.4 was shown to an office of Merrill Lynch advisors January 2009. Using weekly data the crashes of 1987 and 2008

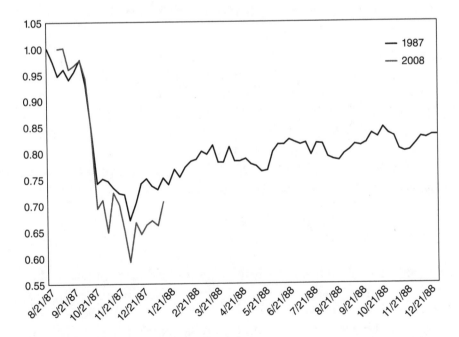

Figure 2.4   October Crashes of 1987 and 2008

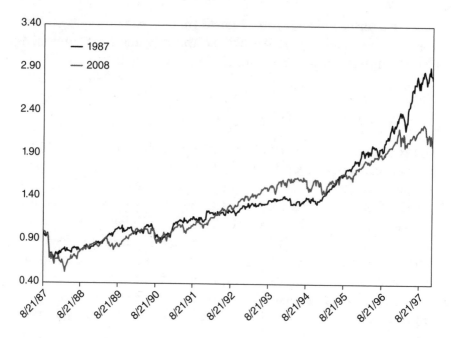

Figure 2.5 S&P 500 Index, Crashes of 1987 and 2008 Nine Years Later

appear similar. It was suggested to the audience that over the next couple of years the market could recover from the 2008 crash like it did following 1987. In other words, we had a post-crash recovery road map.

Figure 2.5 is an update ten years later that shows that the post-crash 1987 recovery was a good road map for the post-crash 2008 recovery. Many times the market got to the same place at the same time after 2008 as it did following 1987.

Summary

This multiyear bull market was sensible and similar to previous bull markets in many aspects. Its annual returns were in line with, and pretty typical of, ninety-five years of returns dating back to 1926. The sector leadership was economically sensitive and cyclical along with a recovery in financials. Volatility was rewarded as high beta stocks were among the leaders. Earnings, and therefore fair value, grew and prices just followed. Typical of previous bull markets, the market dropped about 45% of the trading days. Also, like previous bull markets, big surge days were important contributors. Finally, its recovery from the crash of 2008 was similar to the recovery from the crash of 1987. So as shown in Chapter 1, why did many investors not participate? Why was the multiyear bull market referred to as unloved? The following chapters will address those issues.

Keys to Maximizing Performance from 2009 through 2020

- Believe in the economy.
- Hold cyclical and economically sensitive sectors.
- Believe financials would "right the ship" following the financial crisis.
- Tolerate volatility and hold high beta stocks.
- Participate in surge days.
- Recognize growth in corporate earnings.

Chapter 3
News and Stock Prices

omething very unusual happened at the market peak of
October 2007 as the market was about to begin its seventeen-
month decline. We believe what happened taught a generation of investors an unproductive lesson, especially baby boomers
who are more and more interested in capital preservation. They
learned to sell stocks on the slightest bit of bad news and to believe
bad news predicted a bear market. This behavior did not serve them
well during the post 2009 bull market. As there was a fair amount of
occasional bad news the whole way up the multiyear bull market,
we believe investors incorrectly reacted to it. Before examining that,
let's look at the normal relationship between news and stock prices.

For many decades, the format of the front page of the *Wall Street
Journal* hasn't changed. There are one or two sentences of introduction to articles that appear on various pages throughout the
paper. Research in the mid-1970s rated those first five blurbs as to
whether they were good or bad for business, good getting a plus 1,
bad getting a negative 1. The score could range from plus 5 if all five
articles were good for business to negative 5 if all five articles were
bad for business. They compared the news quality to subsequent
stock returns. Jumping to the summary, they found that investors
should buy stocks when the news is bad and sell stocks when the
news is good.

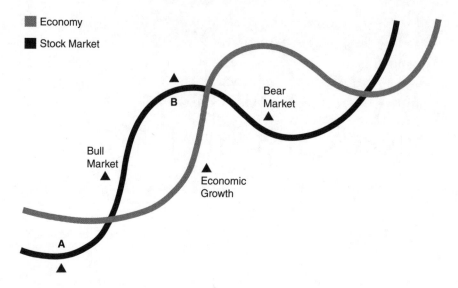

■ Economy

■ Stock Market

Bear
Market
▲

B

Bull
Market
▲

Economic
Growth
▲

A
▲

Figure 3.1   Hypothetical Stock Market and Economy

Here it is schematically (see Figure 3.1). The black line represents the stock market moving left to right through time. It has been shown to lead the economy (gray line) by six to nine months at turning points. At point A the economy and therefore the news are bad and getting worse, yet the stock market turns, rallies, and leads the economy upward. It is difficult for investors to buy when the news is bad and getting worse, but it is normally prudent at major turning points. At the market peak, point B, the economy and news are good and getting better, yet the stock market peaks out and heads lower before the economy turns down. It is difficult for investors to sell when the news is good and getting better but again, it is normally prudent at major turning points.

We passed this concept on to investors in our February 2009 Portfolio Update written about a month before the March bottom. "If historical trends are any indication, the market will typically rebound six to nine months ahead of any general improvement in the economy or popular headlines. As we stated last month, we believe conditions are in place for a possible market advance as 2009 unfolds." Looking back, the market bottom in 2009 was classic and quite similar to point A in Figure 3.1. Stock prices rallied off the March 9 low while the economy continued to worsen for many months.

To show this concept with real data, we use employment as a measure of economic activity and graph employment and the S&P 500 Index quarterly in Figure 3.2. We could have picked any period, but we chose the ten years from 1967 to 1976 because it shows two cycles in ten years. Employment is 1.00 minus unemployment. As an example, if the unemployment rate is 6%, it would appear on the graph as 94% employment. At both tops, 1968 and 1972, the S&P 500 (black) peaked first, headed lower and then employment (gray) followed downward two to three quarters later. At both market bottoms, 1970 and 1974, stocks began their rallies two to three quarters before employment began to improve. These four events are classic with stocks leading the news, in this case employment, by two to three quarters.

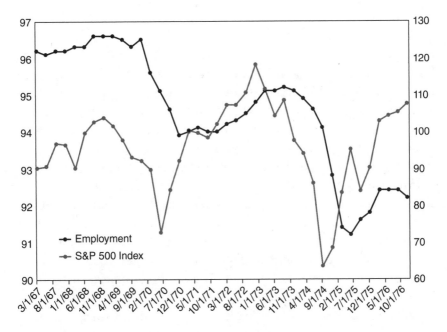

Figure 3.2   Stock Prices and Employment, 1967–1976

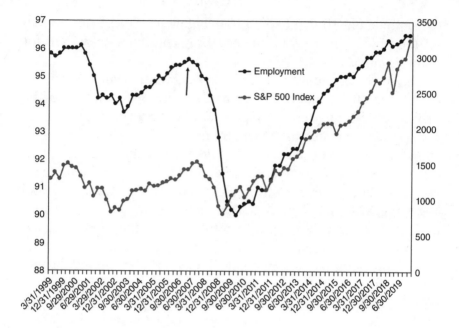

Figure 3.3   Stock Prices and Employment, 1999–2019

Figure 3.3 shows similar timing with stocks leading employment for the downturn of 2000 and the rally of 2002, but look at 2007 (see the arrow). What's unusual is that employment turned down first and led stock prices lower. Investors who reacted to negative news, employment declining, and sold were rewarded. A behavior that is typically punished, selling on bad news, got rewarded. We suspect that at that peak of 2007 and the bear market that followed individual investors performed better than professional money managers who had been trained to expect stocks to lead the economy and its various bits of data. In other words, professionals have been trained to not sell on a month or two of disappointing economic data. Yet selling when employment and presumably other economic variables experienced declines proved productive for investors in 2007.

Notice that at the bottom of 2009 the historically normal relationship of the stock market leading the economy returned. Stocks led the improvement in employment by three quarters, but the damage had been done. A generation of investors had been emboldened with the view they could time the market by selling when the economic news was disappointing and probably waiting to buy when the news turned favorable. In our view, this explains some of the market's behavior and performance during the eleven-year bull market. Many investors missed most of the upside because they were scared off by disappointing economic news and were waiting for good news. Also, we contend investors were quicker than normal to take profits, as we have seen shorter-than-normal industry and sector themes and even theme reversals. Imagine being in an eleven-year bull market and selling when unemployment upticks, housing starts drop a month, or durable goods orders fall slightly. Such short-term reactions to news happened to have helped at the unusual peak of 2007 but proved harmful during the multiyear bull market. We believe those behaviors were occurring and attribute it to the unhealthy lesson learned at the peak of 2007. For the eleven-year bull market, selling on disappointing economic news was not productive but it was a popular behavior—a behavior left over from and learned at the unusual peak of 2007.

Industry-Specific News

We have been focusing on the broad market and how investors may have been waiting for good news before investing. Here is an example of industry-specific news that could have kept investors from participating in a nice move in bank stocks. An article entitled "Bank Profits Dealt Another Blow as Yields Hit Record Lows" in the *Wall Street Journal* on July 5, 2016, by Rachel Louise Ensign suggested problems for bank profits due to a flattening yield curve. "The 10-year Treasury yield fell to 1.367% on Tuesday, the lowest ever. At the same time, the difference between yields on the two-year and 10-year notes fell Tuesday to about 0.81 percentage point, its lowest level in more than eight years." So far, the writer just stated facts, but here comes the opinion. "The continuing downward march in yields is expected to render lending less profitable and drive down the income from securities that banks hold. That, along with the likelihood the Federal Reserve won't raise rates again for the foreseeable future, may pack a potent punch to bank profitability." We can only suppose that a reader seeing this gloomy outlook might have avoided bank stocks. Bad move! From July 5, 2016, to July 5, 2017, one year after that article, the S&P Regional Bank Index gained 54.38% and for the two-year period through July 5, 2018, that index gained 72.26%.

There is a lot going on in this example to show how investors, not just Ms. Ensign, interpreted observations and events and came up with incorrect negative outlooks: (1) assuming a flat yield curve is bad for bank profits, (2) assuming the yield curve will continue to flatten, and (3) guessing what the Fed will do.

The yield curve is a graph of yields for various maturities of Treasury bills, notes, and bonds. The x-axis is time to maturity, ranging from zero to usually thirty years. The y-axis is yield. If there is a big difference between the yield on short-term and long-term bonds the curve is said to be steep. If there is not much of a difference in short-term and long-term yields the curve is said to be flat. From late 2013 through mid-2016, the yield on the 10-year notes had been dropping from nearly 3.0% to about 1.50%, and the yield on the 2-year notes had been inching upward from near 0.3% to about 0.7%. So, the yield curve flattened. The article states the popular view that a flat yield curve is bad for bank profits and is built on the assumption that banks borrow short term (deposits) and lend long term. We don't believe that and instead believe that banks are very good at matching short-term deposits with short-term loans and long-term CDs with long-term loans. We believe there are many variables, conditions, and skills that determine bank profits, not just the yield curve. Chapter 13 will address investors' tendency to believe that one condition totally determines an outcome that is actually a function of many variables. The world is more complicated than A (yield curve) causes B (bank profits).

Another example of human behavior is believing that what has happened recently will continue into the future, as seen in the words, "The continuing downward march in yields . . . ." Projecting

Table 3.1 Yields (%)

	13-Week T-Bill	2-Year Treasury Notes	10-Year Treasury Notes
7/5/2016	0.38	0.55	1.38
7/5/2017	1.06	1.40	2.32
7/5/2018	1.97	2.55	2.83

what happened the last three years out into the future proved wrong. Table 3.1 shows the yields on the 13-week T-Bill and 2-year and 10-year Treasury notes at the time of date of the article, one year and two years later. They didn't march downward; they all rose. The world and things change, usually when you least expect it.

Based on the news and economic conditions at the time of the article we did not believe the Federal Reserve needed to raise the Federal Funds rate and drain reserves. Apparently the author of that article felt the same way and stated, "That, along with the likelihood the Federal Reserve won't raise rates again for the foreseeable future . . ." It is very risky to assume the Federal Reserve (Fed) will do what you think it should do because the Fed has a mind of its own. It raised its target for the Federal Funds rate by 0.25% in December 2016, three times in 2017 and four times in 2018. This was a bad one, two, three combination but not uncommon during the unloved bull market. The yield curve didn't continue to flatten and didn't hurt bank profits. Yields didn't continue marching downward and the Fed raised its Federal Funds target. The S&P Regional Bank Index gained 54.38% one year and 72.26% two years after that article.

Expectations

It seems that the market was back to its normal way of leading the economy and economic news by six to nine months all the way up the eleven-year bull market, but many investors missed the bull market because they were focused on recent or current news. The next chapter will show that the economy was indeed imperfect, and offered plenty of disappointing bits of data along the way but the stock market ultimately chugged its way to all-time highs. Why?

If investors expect the economy to be horrible over the next year and it turns out to just be bad, stocks can rally. If investors expect the economy to be bad and it turns out to be mediocre, stocks can continue rallying. Then if investors expect the economy to be mediocre and it turns out to be good, stocks can continue to rally. The economy never had to be perfect to justify a bull market; it just had to be better than expectations. This was the concept related to Erin Burnet on CNBC on July 13, 2009, as told in the Introduction. The market doesn't need a catalyst to rally. The economy just has to be better than previously feared.

- Usually stock prices lead the economy and economic news.
- The opposite occurred at the peak of 2007, which was very unusual.
- That explains why some investors didn't participate.

Chapter 4
Economic Setting

Following a recession, economists describe the economy as usually going through two phases: recovery then expansion. Economic activity first recovers, sometimes slowly, other times with a surge. Then momentum kicks in and sets the stage for steady expansion (economic growth). Not this time! The post-2008–2009 recession economy was different and imperfect by historic standards and investors' wishes.

Figure 4.1 shows quarter-over-quarter (Q-O-Q) rate of change in gross domestic product (GDP) from the first quarter of 2008 through the fourth quarter of 2019, which closely aligns with the end of the eleven-year bull market. What stands out first is the four sequential quarters of negative GDP, or contraction, third quarter 2008 through second quarter 2009. The first positive quarter-to-quarter growth to start the recovery was the third quarter 2009. For the twenty quarters (five years) beginning with the third quarter of 2009, three quarters were negative and six out of the twenty were .5% or less. The recovery struggled and momentum never kicked in to set the stage for steady expansion until middle to late 2016.

There are a variety of contributors to this imperfect recovery. The behavior of the Fed is one of them. In the next chapter we will show how the Fed stimulated growth of the money supply to promote recovery but then quickly slowed it down due to inflation fears.

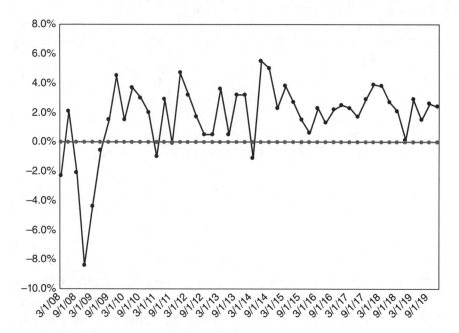

Figure 4.1 Quarter-Over-Quarter GDP, 3/2008–12/2019 DGP

As we now know, those inflation fears were inappropriate. The Fed slowed the growth of the money supply before economic momentum was established and inhibited the economy from moving from recovery to expansion. A year later, the Fed had to employ a second round of monetary expansion known as QE2.

With GDP declining in three of those early twenty quarters and growing less than 0.5% in three others, there was enough economic disappointment for skeptics to keep their money on the sidelines, contributing to, as we mentioned before, the "unloved" nature of the bull market. There was a reoccurring, if not constant, concern that the economy would fall back into recession. The "two steps forward, one step back" nature of this recovery caused many observers to doubt its sustainability.

Predictions of a "double-dip" recession were frequently offered by economists. For example, in the *Wall Street Journal* on October 6, 2010, three economists offered concerns about the economy heading back into recession. "We are probably debating words at this point; a secondary dip is playing out," said Paul Ballew, chief economist at Nationwide. And in agreement, "The economy has already been hit by a series of shocks earlier this year, so I think we need just one more modest shock to tip the economy back into recession," said Bank of America economist Michelle Meyer. And a third view for good measure, "This puts a double dip back on the table," said Justin Wolfers, an economist at the University of Pennsylvania's Wharton School.

As seen in the first chapter, the ICON valuation readings indicated stocks were underpriced during the early years of recovery. In an attempt to persuade financial advisors and investors to our bullish posture we poked some fun at the predictors of the double-dip recession. In 2011, we wrote, "A double-dip recession is a largely mythical economic creature that has rarely been seen or measured by humans. Some contend a double-dip recession was last experienced between 1980 and 1982. In any event, the term 'double-dip recession' is quite real to people prone to worry about things that may never come to be." Despite our best efforts at coaxing, we suspect we were unable to dissuade their negative view of the economy.

Europe

Europe experienced an even more sluggish, less consistent recovery from the great recession, which was a drag on global growth and contributed to the imperfect recovery in the United States. Figure 4.2 shows the Q-O-Q GDP growth for France and Germany. Both countries experienced the global recession with France's being longer (five quarters of negative GDP) whereas Germany's was deeper (−4.5% first quarter 2009). Both countries experienced recovery surges initially but then settled back into disappointing and frequently interrupted growth. Let's note the number of quarters with 0.2% or less growth because four straight quarters of only 0.2% growth would not even reach a dismal 1% for an annual rate. From second quarter 2011 through third quarter 2016 France had fourteen of those twenty-two quarters with Q-O-Q GDP growth of

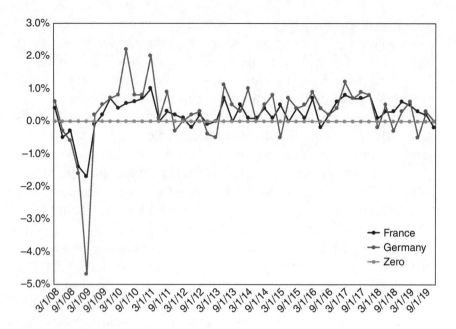

Figure 4.2   Quarter-Over-Quarter GDP 3/08–12/19

0.2% or less including three that were negative. During that same period Germany experienced eight quarters with 0.2% or less Q-O-Q growth with four of those being negative.

As we will show in the next chapter, the European Central Bank (ECB) stimulated growth in its money supply, which explains the initial recovery surge, but then pulled back, presumably due to inflation fears. This focus on inflation prevention is understandable because, unlike in the United States, where our Federal Reserve has the dual mandate of full employment and price stability, the ECB has only one mandate: price stability. Just as in the United States, the European economies never went from the standard recovery to expansion, making Europe a drag on the global economy.

China

China's influence on the global economic recovery can best be seen in Figure 4.3, which shows year-over-year (Y-O-Y) GDP on a

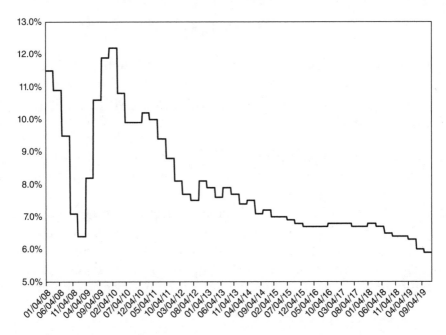

Figure 4.3   China Year-Over-Year GDP, 2008–2019

quarterly basis. At the peak of the last economic expansion in 2006 and 2007, Y-O-Y GDP was in the 12% to 14% range for China. During the global recession, China did experience a significant slowdown to 6.4%. As will be seen in the next chapter it used monetary easing to help jolt its economy, and the global economy as well, to recovery.

Monetary stimulus worked as China experienced growth back up over 12%, but then there must have been some heated debates. Some in power must have argued, "Why are we risking inflation to stimulate other economies?" In other words, "Why are we pulling the global economic train?" You can see what must have been a deliberate, orchestrated slowing of the growth of their economy from 2011 through 2019. Our US economy not only didn't have a vigorous European expansion to help but also didn't have the 12% to 14% growth in China that it benefited from during the previous expansion. There were a lot of people in the recovery boat, but many were not paddling.

Economic Surprises

Citigroup Global Markets computes and distributes an index they call The Citi Surprise Index. They survey economists and analysts to get their forecasts for a variety of variables. Then Citigroup compares the forecasts to the actual data when they are released. The index measures data surprises relative to market expectations. A positive reading means that the data releases have been stronger than expected and a negative reading means that the data releases have been worse than expected.

Figure 4.4 shows the Citi Economic Surprise Index weekly from January 2, 2009, through February 21, 2020. The first thing that stands out is the predictions are like a broken clock, correct twice a day. The next thing that stands out is how they rapidly fluctuate from better than expected to worse than expected. It appears that when released data are worse than expected the forecasters

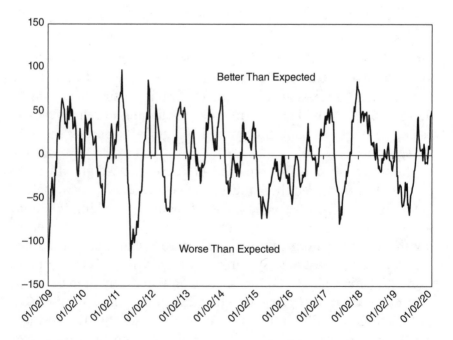

Figure 4.4   Citi Economic Surprise Index

revise their forecasts downward, too far downward. It appears they compensate too much. Then the released data become better than their downwardly revised forecasts, so they revise their forecasts upward, eventually too far upward. And so on, back and forth. This cycle repeats, much to the dismay of the investor and money managers using economic forecasts for investment guidance.

Perhaps the rapid reversals are just human nature and not unique to economists. In the 1990s, we did an investment presentation to an audience in Torrance, California, which included many aerospace engineers. We were stating how a disciplined value approach to investing can filter out the news and investors' tendency to react, or more often than not, overreact, to the news. A fellow in the audience raised his hand and said in aviation that is known as "pilot-induced oscillation." If the plane's nose is up, the pilot turns it down, but perhaps too much. Then the pilot tends to turn the nose up too much. Pretty soon the plane is on a path resembling the Citi Economic Surprise Index.

So maybe it is human nature for economic forecasters to "over-revise," but it is likely that the two steps forward, one step back nature of the economic recovery caused forecasters' fits. It just appears forecasters had a difficult time getting their arms around the imperfect recovery. Perhaps this economist-induced oscillation contributed to investors holding cash and not fully participating in the multiyear bull market.

Summary

Throughout this bull market, many objections to being invested seemed to come at us from the thirty-thousand-foot level, based on a macroeconomic view. We would respond to those objections by saying that the boots on the ground, company-by-company analysis dictated being invested. There were healthy, growing companies at attractive prices. This dichotomy between the macroeconomic and company analysis levels will be discussed more in Chapter 12. We will see that managers who start their investment process with an economic forecast did not do very well during the eleven-year bull market. Managers who were simply looking for rapidly growing companies or well-managed companies with a dominant brand, which were easy to find, performed very well. Not paying attention to the imperfect economy proved to be advantageous.

A few things contributed to investors not fully participating in the great, but unloved, bull market. With regard to the economic setting, the domestic economy frequently either retreated or experienced sluggish growth. Europe weighed on the US economy because recoveries in those countries were even weaker and less consistent than in the United States. China chose to lower its GDP growth, which diminished its contribution to global growth. The result was an economy that economists and investors alike just couldn't figure out, which kept many investors from participating or maximizing returns in the great bull market.

- During this period there was recovery but no robust expansion.
- Europe was a drag.
- China was slower than in the past.
- There were problems for economic forecasters.

Chapter 5

Inflation and Interest Rates

F igure 5.1 shows the twelve-month rate of change for the Consumer Price Index (CPI) from January 1970 to April 2021. At the left, it can be seen how quickly inflation accelerated in the 1970s, especially from 1977 to 1980. The peak was March 1980 at 14.8%. What may surprise many is how quickly it was reduced. Disinflation took only about three years, from that peak in March 1980 to August 1983, when it was tamed to a docile 2.6% over the previous twelve months. Since January 1983, as measured by the CPI, inflation has averaged only 2.64% over all of the rolling twelve-month periods through April 2021 (straight line). Disinflation wasn't a twenty- or thirty-year process; it took three years. There have been spurts of inflation since 1983 but nothing significant or sustainable. From the graph it seems so obvious that inflation was tamed and nothing to worry about.

Yet investors kept worrying about inflation returning. We have been doing presentations to financial advisor and investor audiences since 1991. The most frequent objection to owning stocks and bonds the entire time has been the fear that inflation was coming back and, therefore, interest rates were going higher. Those

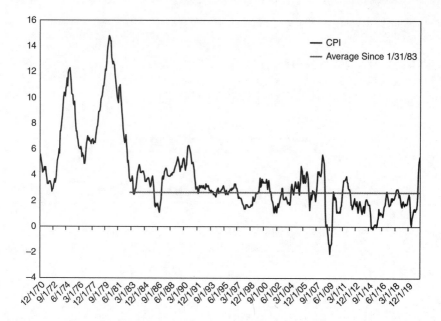

Figure 5.1   Twelve-Month Rolling CPI Rate of Change, 1/1970–6/2021

concerns have persisted during the recent multiyear bull market and kept many investors in cash. As evidence we point to mortgage brokers who have been successfully appealing to that fear by stating, "Refinance your home now before interest rates go higher." That pitch worked by playing on people's persistent fears of increasing inflation and interest rates.

This first example of a predisposition to predict inflation is from June 2009, right near the bottom of the recession. With high unemployment you'd think the last thing to worry about would be inflation. Yet, in a *Wall Street Journal* article on June 8, 2009, entitled, "Land Mines Pockmark Road to Recovery," Mark Gongloff wrote, "But the market for U.S. Treasury debt had its worst day in nine months, driven by worries about inflation and higher interest rates." Then, two paragraphs later he went on a roll of conjecture, basically saying the side effects of inflation could halt the economic recovery. Because he was "preaching to the choir" (investors who feared inflation) it probably made sense to investors at that time.

"A jump in economic growth, for example, could send commodity prices sharply higher. On Friday, oil briefly traded above $70 a barrel, due partly to economic optimism. Worries about inflation would cause interest rates to rise, hurting the housing market. Higher commodity prices could also be a drag on economic recovery, pushing job losses higher and leading to more mortgage defaults." Wow! Doomsday, all because of inflation. Looking back, we now know inflation remained low and interest rates dropped.

Here is another example of expectations for higher interest rates, five years into the bull market, in an article in *Fortune*, June 14, 2014, entitled "The Real Reason Interest Rates Are Rising," by Nin-Hai Tseng. "A curious thing is happening with interest rates. Since the financial crisis, the cost of borrowing have sunk to historic lows . . . But that's changing as rates are rising again." . . . "And yet, as investors brace for what some say could be a new era of higher interest rates, global markets in bonds, currencies and stocks have experienced bouts of turmoil." The presumption of higher interest rates proved incorrect. On Friday June 13, 2014, the day before the article appeared, the yield on the 10-year Treasury note was 2.604%. About seven months later, on January 30, 2015, it had dropped to 1.642%. As for short-term interest rates, the yield on the 13-week T-Bill was 0.084% on Friday June 13, 2014. It dropped to 0.032 % by September. A year after that article about rising rates the yield on the 13-week had inched up to only 0.091%.

A few more quotes from 2014 can help get a feel for how prevailing the expectations for higher interest rates were. On September 29, 2014, *Bloomberg News* reported, "Some of the world's most successful money managers say bonds are due for a tumble. Julian Robertson, the billionaire founder of Tiger Management LLC, said at the Bloomberg Markets Most Influential Summit this month that there's a bubble in bonds that will end 'in a very bad way.'" Omega Advisors Inc. founder Leon Cooperman called bonds "very overvalued" and Howard Marks, the chairman of Oaktree Capital Group LLC, said interest rates are "unnaturally low." In summary, these comments are saying bonds were priced too high and their yields were too low. A couple of weeks later on October 10, 2014,

Bloomberg News reported, "Primary dealers had the biggest short position on benchmark government notes at the beginning of the month since last year's taper tantrum. It was the wrong bet: The debt has gained 1.5 percent in October as 10-year Treasury yields plunged to the lowest since June 2013." Short positions in bonds are bets that prices will drop and yields will rise. The article continued, "'Over the last year, what's sort of been the market's focus is everyone is bearish,' preparing for rates to rise, said David Ader, head of interest-rate strategy at CRT Capital Group LLC." A bubble in bonds? Overvalued bonds? Interest rates "unnaturally low"? Primary dealers short selling bonds? Looking back, all wrong but reflecting the intuitive, but incorrect, belief that interest rates should rise.

Stuck in the 1970s

In response to the questions about inflation and higher interest rates, we have offered data, graphs, charts, and logic to support the case for disinflation and lower interest rates. In hindsight, even though we were correct, the audiences never seemed fully convinced, because their gut feelings overruled the data, graphs, and charts we presented. We contend that the fear of returning inflation and higher interest rates is the biggest generational miss we will see, all a residual of the inflation jolt of the late 1970s.

Women have been known to observe that men stick with the haircut they had during what they remember to be the best years of their lives, whereas women often change their hairstyle. The inflation jolt of the late 1970s had a big impact on a generation and fixed their "economic hairstyle" on inflation and higher interest rates. Here is an example of how the Great Depression did the same thing to another generation. My father graduated from high school in 1931 during the Great Depression. Besides extremely high unemployment the depression also caused thousands of bank failures. My father never trusted banks and always carried an unusual amount of cash with him in case his bank would fail. Just as the depression of the 1930s molded a generation's views on banking, the inflation jolt of the 1970s did the same on young people of that era.

A similar view was stated in a *Bloomberg Businessweek,* September 23, 2019, article titled "Why We Love to Call Everything a Bubble" by Joe Weisenthal. He described Helene Meisler as a stock market columnist who's been active in the market for four decades and then quoted her, "I have often thought that we are all products of when we 'grew up' in the market. So, for example, folks who grew up in the '70s are always looking for inflation. Those who grew up in the '80s are always on alert for a crash."

Phony, Fabricated, and Dangerous

How did the fear of inflation returning and interest rates rising affect investor behavior during the recent multiyear bull market? If a person has a powerful gut feel–based expectation that inflation will return and interest rates will rise, what does that person do when the opposite happens? The Fed eased monetary policy, but inflation, instead of increasing, dropped to 2%. Along with it, T-Bills went to near zero and the ten-year Treasury yield dropped below 2% when the investor expected inflation at 4%, T-Bills at 4%, and the ten-year Treasury yield near 6%. We found ourselves in a completely opposite world, in terms of inflation and interest rates, than most investors expected.

What do you do? Well, the investor could admit being wrong, but most couldn't. It is easier for investors to say the world is wrong than to admit their intuitive-based forecast was wrong. Instead, they reasoned that this new setting was phony, fabricated, and dangerous because it disagreed with their gut feeling. What would an investor do who thought the interest rate setting was phony, fabricated, and dangerous? Probably be cautious and even sell stocks and watch stock prices move higher while sitting on the sidelines.

Here is an example, from an advisory letter. The author (Carl) did very well over the years for himself and his followers by analyzing individual stock situations. He continues to write market and economic commentary to his followers, which requires a totally different skill set that he lacks. On February 10, 2020, he wrote, "The stock market has surprised me over the last two years. I did not expect interest rates to remain down as long as they have." Over the two years leading up to that writing, the S&P 1500 Index gained 31.2%. Apparently he missed that impressive gain because of an expectation that interest rates would not remain low but would increase. He is not alone because the view that low interest rates were phony, fabricated, and dangerous was quite common.

Negative Interest Rates

In the later years of the eleven-year unloved bull market negative interest rates appeared. Investors had never seen them before. As just stated, in a setting where some investors thought low interest rates were phony, fabricated, and dangerous, negative interest rates just added fuel to that fire. In November 2016, we wrote a paper to address that topic and essentially to tell investors not to worry about them.

That was November 2016. The bull market continued, charging on despite negative interest rates. We assume investors owning those "negative rate" bonds wished they had owned stocks instead.

Negative Interest Rates Explained . . . And Not So Scary

November 3, 2016

As interest rates continue through their recent secular thirty-five year downward trend—which we have labeled as the return to the old normal—we now encounter something not seen before: negative interest rates. Unfamiliar with negative interest rates, the financial media and many investors seem baffled and even frightened by them. We have seen descriptions and references to negative interest rates that seem incorrect to us. For example, "investors are paying Germany to hold their money," which implies that Germany is issuing bonds and investors are paying Germany interest. Such a description may have intuitive appeal but is, in our opinion, incorrect. It has also been portrayed that the European Central Bank (ECB) and the Bank of Japan (BOJ) are causing the negative rates and using them as a tool for implementing their monetary policy. True, the central banks are charging member banks to hold reserve deposits, but we think the label of "negative rates" is incorrect.

Let's begin with bond mathematics 101. If an issuer issues a bond with a $20 annual coupon and will pay back the face value of $1,000 in ten years, an investor requiring a return of 2.0% per year will be willing to pay $1,000 (face value) for the bond. Table 5.1 shows the annual payments of $20 and the $1,000 face value being discounted at 2.0%. The present value of those future payments adds to $1,000.

Table 5.1 Bond Valuation Basics

Year	Payment	Present Value
1	$20	$19.61
2	$20	$19.22
3	$20	$18.85
4	$20	$18.48
5	$20	$18.11
6	$20	$17.76
7	$20	$17.41
8	$20	$17.07
9	$20	$16.74
10	$20	$16.41
10	$1,000	$820.35

(continued)

(continued)

If instead, an investor paid $1,211.16 for the bond, the yield to maturity would be −.1%, a situation labeled lately as negative interest rates. The investor would still receive the $20 interest payments each year but would suffer capital depreciation of $211.16 over the ten-year life of the bond. The bond holder is not paying the issuer interest payments. In fact there is a current yield of 1.65% ($20/$1,211.16). The bond buyer is simply willing to pay so much more for the bond ($1,211.16) than the $1,000 face value that will be repaid at maturity.

Why would speculators or investors be doing this? Speculators may buy the bonds with a short-term horizon, such as one month, hoping that somebody will be willing to pay more than $1211.16. Bond prices and yields are determined in the open market by supply and demand. On the demand side, investors might be willing to own a bond with a negative yield to maturity if they did not like alternatives like equities, real estate, precious metals, or other commodities. Their willingness to accept a negative yield to maturity would seem to reflect a dislike for risky investments combined with an expectation for low inflation or even deflation.

As for policy, we disagree with the notion that central banks or governments are using negative interest rates as a tool. In the United States, the Federal Reserve (Fed) historically did not pay member banks on reserve deposits with the Fed. Over the last few years, that changed and the Fed has been paying interest on the deposits. In Europe and Japan, the central bank is charging member banks interest to hold reserve deposits. There is nothing "negative" in this arrangement. We think of it as a nudge, or slight penalty, if banks are holding excess reserves and not making the maximum amount of loans possible.

We have heard it stated, "negative interest rates aren't working," which implies controlling interest rates is the primary tool being used by the central banks. We believe the monetary policy tool for central banks is the rate of growth of their money supply, not interest rates. The central bank adds or reduces bank reserves, banks increase or decrease their lending, and the growth of the money supply increases or decreases. Interest rates are just a byproduct, based on the supply of money and demand for money.

We have an explanation for why investors and the financial media are so concerned, worried, and skeptical of today's low and negative interest rate environment and it has to do with expectation versus reality. Ever since the peak in interest rates in October 1981, there has been a popular and steady, but incorrect, prediction of higher inflation and higher interest rates. Perhaps those pundits thought the conditions of the late 1970s were normal. Whenever we hear someone call for higher interest rates, we joke that he or she sound just like the people who were wrong five, ten, fifteen, twenty, twenty-five, and thirty years ago. They all said the same thing and gave the same reasons. We can only guess that for the large group that have been predicting higher rates, today's low rates are very uncomfortable and even baffling. It would seem to be easier just to admit that previous forecasts were wrong.

The global economy is in a low-growth setting with minimal, if any, inflationary pressures and most governments unwilling to provide fiscal stimulus. Low and negative interest rates are not fabricated or artificial, but are the result of the overall setting and are not something to worry about.

Why Didn't the Easy Monetary Policy Ignite Inflation?

Think of inflation as compounding price increase on top of price increase on top of price increase and so on. A one-time price increase is not inflation.

The inflation jolt of the 1970s took about twenty to thirty variables to all line up and fall in place. The large baby boomer generation needed starter housing, along with other goods and services not already there for them. They demanded goods and services immediately. Price was no problem, so prices went higher and higher. On the flip side as a young workforce, they were demanding and even belligerent. Workers in their twenties are much more likely to go on strike than workers in their forties and fifties, who value security. Oil prices had risen with OPEC rising in its strength and power. The list, which formed a perfect storm for inflation, goes on and on, and as stated, it probably meant twenty to thirty variables all lining up. We have not had all those conditions lining up the last few decades, maybe one or two here and there, but not all together. Over the last three decades, if a company raised its price, the executive would hide under the desk hoping the price increase held. During this multiyear bull market the foundations for inflation were not in place, yet stuck in the 1970s, investors continually worried about it.

Capacity Utilization

We were at a conference in Phoenix a couple of years into the recovery, and after our presentation a financial advisor came up with the familiar view that inflation was returning and interest rates were going higher. He reasoned that the expansive monetary policy would fuel inflation. He even issued a statement he had probably memorized for a college economics exam, "too many dollars, chasing too few goods." The problem with his reasoning was that there was not "too few goods." At that time and still today, we can make more of anything we want. There are no shortages, which fuel price increases. You want more software or hardware? No problem. You want more blue jeans, windows, roof tile, or automobiles? No problem. We can make more of anything. It should be noted that in spring and summer 2021, there were some shortages in a few products such as semiconductors and lumber, but that appears to be more a function of businesses being surprised by the robust economic recovery than long-term capacity issues.

Figure 5.2 shows capacity utilization 1967 to 2021. Capacity utilization tracks the extent to which the installed productive capacity of a country is being used in the production of goods and services. It drops sharply during recessions: 1969, 1974, 1982, 2001, 2008, and 2020. Those aside, it has been trending downward the last few

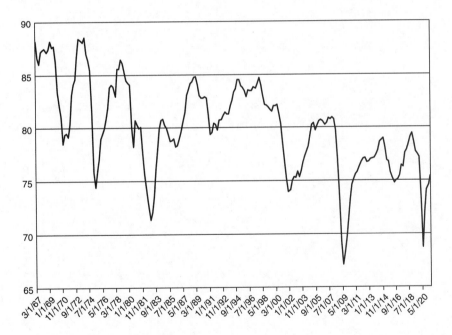

Figure 5.2 Capacity Utilization

decades. During the eleven-year bull market, it was in the 75% to 79% range, whereas in the 1970s it was over 85% at peaks. It is difficult for inflation to get a toehold when there is excess capacity for production and therefore no shortages.

2009 Outlook

In 2009, we put out a short research report on inflation. It showed how recessions reduce inflation. We made the case that inflation could stay low for a few years following 2009.

Inflation Following a Recession

June 9, 2009

Ever since the inflation jolt of the late 1970s, investors have worried about higher rates of inflation returning. Yet, since 1982 inflation, as measured by the Consumer Price Index (CPI), has averaged a very moderate and tolerable 3% per year.

Today, again, we hear concerns raised because of the monetary and fiscal stimulus being thrown at the economy. So we looked into previous recessions and their impact on future inflation. It appears recessions have a powerful dampening effect on inflation.

For each of the previous four recessions, 1974, 1982, 1991, and 2001, we computed the average CPI rate of change the previous two years (Table 5.2). Even though recessions do not match exactly with calendar years, we used CPI change for those periods. Then we computed an average annual change in the CPI for the subsequent four years.

For example, for 1972 and 1973, inflation averaged 10.50% per year. Then for the four-year period of 1974 through 1977, inflation averaged 6.91% per year. The

Table 5.2   Consumer Price Index (CPI) before and after a Recession

Year	1974	1982	1991	2001	Average	2008
CPI Previous Two Years	10.50%	10.67%	4.59%	3.04%	7.20%	3.32%
CPI Subsequent Four Years	6.91%	3.85%	2.72%	2.27%	3.93%	1.96%*
Percent Reduction in CPI	–34.2%	–63.9%	–40.8%	–25.3%	–41.1%	

Based on a reduction of 41.1%

recession reduced the rate of inflation by 34.2% for a substantial period of four years. On average over those four recession, there was a 41% reduction in the inflation rate for the next four years. The largest percentage reduction was in the 1982 recession, which was the worst recession of these four with unemployment reaching 11%.

For 2006 and 2007, the inflation rate averaged 3.32%. If we experience the same average reduction this time, inflation will average only 1.96% per year for 2008 through 2011.

SUMMARY—While there are obvious negative consequences of recession, one positive aspect seems to be the repeated ability to reduce inflation significantly over a lengthy four-year period. We can only guess at the reasons. Perhaps workers become more docile in their wage demands. Perhaps coming out of recession businesses try to regain market share rather than raise prices. Other explanations could involve capacity utilization or buyers' abilities to secure favorable long-term contracts during recessions. Anyway, based on past recessions, inflation should remain controlled for a few years.

That report, written and distributed in mid-2009, proved correct because inflation remained low. The average annual increase in the CPI for 2008 through 2011 was even lower than the 1.96% predicted. It was 1.78%. Even through 2018 it was 1.63%. Indeed, the recession of 2008–2009 did knock down inflation just as previous recessions had done, which created a very forgiving setting for monetary expansion.

Velocity of Money

The monetarist school of economics has an equation to explain total spending: $MV = PQ$, where M is the money supply, V is the velocity of money (or the number of times that a dollar turns over), P is the general level of prices, and Q is the quantity of goods and services acquired. The left side says that total spending is the amount of dollars times the number of times they turn over. The right side defines total spending as the price of goods and services times the quantity.

If the money supply is increased and velocity stays constant something on the right side has to increase. Either prices increase or we increase the output of goods and services or some combination of the two. During the recovery from the 2009 recession the Fed promoted growth in the money supply. In the next chapter it will be shown that at times the money supply was experiencing 20% Y-O-Y growth. So why didn't the growth of the money supply cause higher inflation? Let's look at Figure 5.3, which shows the velocity of money from 1959 to 2021.

As discussed, there was excess capacity for production so the Q, or quantity part of the $MV = PQ$, could grow. But another funny thing happened on the way to recovery. The velocity of money declined as seen in the chart of Bloomberg Velocity of M1 1959 to 2021. At the economic peak late 2007, a dollar turned over 10.68 times, but then turnover dropped over the next eleven years to just 5.51 times. Velocity of money slowed and there was excess capacity to produce goods and services. Net result: no or minimal inflation.

Finally, velocity fell off a cliff in 2020 to slightly greater than 1.00 with the self-imposed economic shutdown and recession.

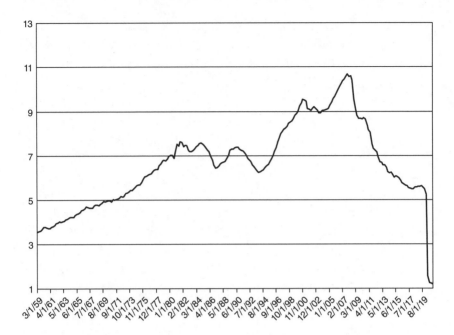

Figure 5.3   Velocity of M1 (Money Supply), 1929–2021

The Fed increased the money supply but in the stay-at-home world, consumers weren't spending. From 2007, velocity of money has dropped from around 10 to 5 to 1. There are some theories as to why it has dropped. One points to the increasing wealth gap over that time between the most wealthy and the lower and middle incomes. It states that the lower and middle incomes spend most or all of their income, whereas the most wealthy do not. Another theory points to the large population of baby boomers, who don't spend like they used to. It is beyond the scope of this book to explain the decrease in velocity. We just believe it was a contributing factor to keeping inflation very low.

Are Low Interest Rates Rational and Normal?

In a letter to investors in January 2013, we wrote, "Currently, we do not see pressure for interest rates to rise significantly. In fact, we believe rates can remain low for many years." Then, regarding stocks, we concluded, "The stock market has just about recovered its losses from the bear market and recession of 2008 and 2009. We believe it is only about halfway through an advance that will take it to new highs."

What was the basis for the belief that "we believe rates can remain low for many years?" It was based on the view that the expectation for inflation is the primary determinant of long-term interest rates. With our expectation that inflation would remain low it followed that interest rates would remain low.

Figure 5.4 shows the yield on Moody's AAA bond index for year-end 1929 to 2020. The chart is dominated by the ascent to the peak in 1981 when investors saw inflation increasing, followed by the thirty-nine-year decline as investors gradually realized disinflation was prevailing. What's normal? We believe the settings for the ascent and decline are unusual and the low steady periods are normal. In 1934, the yield dropped below 4.00% and stayed below

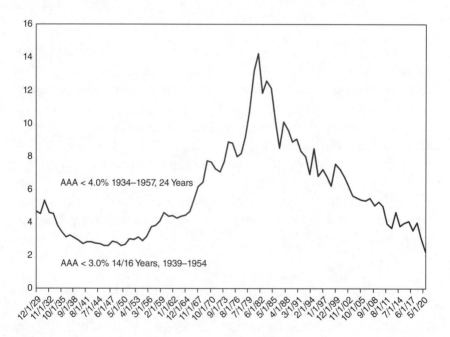

Figure 5.4   Moody's AAA Bond Yield, 1929–2020

4.00% for twenty-four years, 1934 to 1957. In 1939, the yield dropped below 3.00% and stayed below 3.00% for fourteen of the next sixteen years, 1939 to 1954. So rates can go low and stay low for many years, a condition we labeled "the old normal."

Summary

At various times during the bull market when the Fed promoted rapid growth in the money supply many investors expected high inflation would result. Fearing higher inflation, and the resulting higher interest rates, would hurt stocks, they sold and got out of the multiyear bull market. We contend their reasoning was influenced by the fear of inflation left over from the 1970s. Then, when inflation and interest rates went opposite of their expectations, they reasoned the setting was dangerous, resulting in mistrust and more selling of equities. If they could have just realized that low inflation was sensible, they could have also realized that low interest rates were sensible. Instead, gut feel and intuition prevailed, the bull market was unloved, and many investors missed out on the opportunity to accumulate greater wealth the easy way.

- There was a powerful gut-feel expectation for inflation and rising interest rates.
- Unexpected low interest rates must have seemed phony, fabricated, and dangerous
- Negative interest rates cause no problems.
- There was a capacity to produce more, with no shortages.
- Recessions lower inflation.
- Velocity of money declined.
- Low interest rates were sensible and rational.

Chapter 6

The Federal Reserve and Monetary Policy

L et's begin this chapter with a phrase you may have heard or read during the bull market. In a *Bloomberg Businessweek* article, August 12, 2019, Christina Lindblad wrote, "But the government controls the dollar printing press, so it can't go bust." You may have heard such an expression from professional money managers who thought the low interest rates were phony, fabricated, and dangerous and believed that the expansive monetary policy would ignite inflation. They would state "the Government is just printing money." Of course that statement is totally wrong. The Fed is not part of the government. Think of it as a club that banks join. It was intentionally designed to be separate from the government. Through monetary policy, it can influence the growth of the money supply, which is defined to be currency and demand deposits (checking accounts). The US Treasury Department, which is part of the federal government, prints currency and mints coins and has nothing to do with increasing or decreasing the money supply. The Federal Reserve is not the government. The Treasury does not control the money supply. Now that we know that the government does not print (increase the supply of) money, let's see what the Fed does and what role it played in the bull market.

The Federal Reserve was created in 1913. With regard to monetary policy, it has two, sometimes conflicting, mandates of full employment and price stability. In other words, we want people working but we don't want inflation. Its primary tool for implementing this policy is to control the growth of the money supply. If the Fed sells T-Bills to banks, it drains reserves, banks slow down their lending, and the growth of the money supply slows. Just the opposite if the Fed buys T-Bills from banks; it adds reserves, banks increase their lending, and the growth of the money supply increases. As we saw in Chapter 5 and the $MV = PQ$ equation, overall economic activity is influenced by the money supply.

Money Supply

Figure 6.1 shows the fifty-two-week rate of change for M1, the money supply, from December 1979 to February 2020. Each of

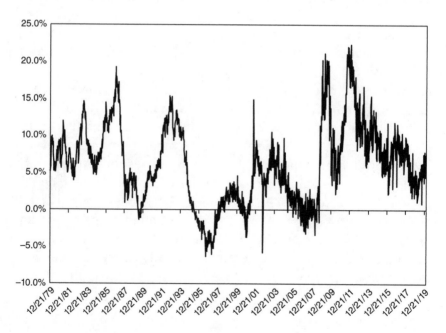

Figure 6.1   M1 Rolling Fifty-Two-Week Percentage Change

the 2,098 observations is simply M1 on that date compared to M1 fifty-two weeks prior. Over this entire period the average fifty-two-week rate of growth is 6.1%. At times when the Fed is pursuing "easy" monetary policy M1 has grown at 10%, 15%, even 20% Y-O-Y. At times when the Fed is pursuing "tight" monetary policy growth, M1 has been slowed to zero or even negative growth.

Figure 6.2 shows the fifty-two-week rate of growth of M1 but just for 2005 through February 2020. Before looking at the money supply during the recovery and bull market, let's focus on 2005–2009. The Fed was so determined to fight inflation that it took the rate of growth in M1 to zero and even negative. When it became aware of subprime mortgage problems summer 2007, the Fed attempted to ease. In August 2007, it lowered the rate at the Discount Window 50 basis points, a more aggressive move than the usual 25-basis-point cut in the Federal Funds rate. Usually, this would inject reserves into the system, banks would lend, and M1 would grow, but not this time.

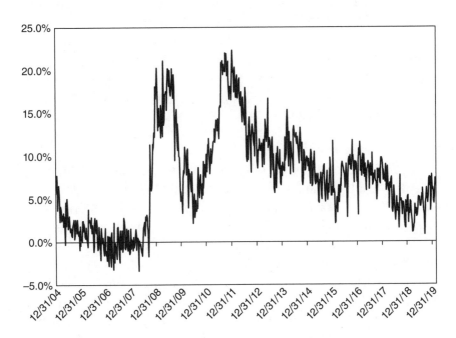

Figure 6.2   M1 Rolling Fifty-Two-Week Percentage Change, 1/05–2/20

The banking system was frozen, a state the Fed (along with the FDIC and Comptroller of the Currency) had failed to pick up in bank examinations. The housing and real estate collapse hit banks from two sides. Banks had made real estate loans but also bought real estate bonds and mortgage-backed securities in their bond portfolios apparently reaching for yield in a low interest rate environment. By frozen, we mean the banks could not make loans. The Fed injected reserves but the banks could not lend so M1 could not grow. Once the Fed realized the circumstances, you saw some unusual actions from the Fed and the Treasury Department trying to unlock the banking system. Terms such as "bailouts" and "too big to fail" were heard frequently as officials would sweep in over a weekend and merge an unhealthy commercial or investment bank into a healthy one. Finally, they succeeded at unlocking the banking system and by late 2008 and early 2009, a year and a half later, banks made loans and M1 grew 20% Y-O-Y.

One final note on what caused the Great Recession is in order, especially when there was so much blame being thrown around. We do not have to look any further than the money supply. If we asked economists, a profession known for disagreement, "what would happen if the growth of M1 went to near zero and even negative for four years?" We expect they would agree and the answer would be, "You'd have a really bad recession!" That is all it would take. The Fed didn't plan on it being four years of no M1 growth but it turned out being that long because the banking system was frozen.

The big spike in the rate of growth of the money supply in early 2009 is a result of banks lending once again. When a bank makes a loan, money is created. Spotting the increase in the money supply we wrote to investors "the cavalry is on the way," meaning the stock market and the economy can recover. Of course, the doubters brought us the old expression that the relationship between increasing the money supply and subsequent economic activity is like pushing on a string. That ineffective relationship did hold in the 1930s with 25% unemployment and massive bank failures, but not in 2009. Once the banking system was unfrozen, M1 grew, the stock market rallied, and then with the usual lag, the economy recovered.

For the Fed governors with the gut level fear that inflation could return (discussed in Chapter 5) 20% Y-O-Y growth in M1 was uncomfortable. Here is an example in a *Wall Street Journal* article by Deborah Lynn Blumberg on February 24, 2011, titled "Fed's Bullard Proposes Inflation Target." "In the current climate of concerns about rising global inflation, it might make sense for the Federal Reserve to set a target for inflation, St. Louis Federal Reserve President James Bullard said Thursday. The Fed is charged with controlling U.S. inflation, but perhaps global inflation will drive U.S. prices higher or cause other problems, he said."

Apparently those who held that view prevailed in meetings and the Fed slowed the growth in the money supply back down to below 5% per year, as seen in Figure 6.2, but the economy had not picked up momentum. It had not transitioned from recovery to expansion. With slower monetary growth, the recovery sputtered, so the Fed reversed course and juiced up the growth of M1 again under the name of Quantitative Easing round 2, or QE2. The Fed's misguided fear of inflation explains the erratic recovery discussed in Chapter 3 and could be a reason for the lack of participation by investors in the multiyear bull market.

There were always doubters who did not believe the easing by the Fed would help the economy. As mentioned, in 2009 they used the "like pushing on a string" analogy. Again in 2011, there were similar doubts expressed about the ability of QE2 to stimulate the economy in the *Wall Street Journal* on September 22, 2011. In an article entitled "Asian Shares, Currencies Plunge," by Alex Frangos, Norman Chan, executive director of the Hong Kong Monetary Authority, questioned the efficacy of the Fed's move. "As the U.S. housing markets are still extremely weak, and U.S. families' debt ratio remains high, it's uncertain how effective the Fed's new measure would be to the U.S. economy." Perhaps Mr. Chan wasn't familiar with an old Wall Street expression, "Don't fight the Fed." It means if the Fed is easing, you want to own stocks. It certainly held valid during this bull market.

Europe and China

The central banks of Europe and China report their money supply monthly. Figure 6.3 shows twelve-month rates of growth for the money supplies of Europe and China for January 2008 through February 2020. Similar to the United States, they both increased the rate of growth of the money supply to stimulate their economies out of the global 2008–2009 recession. They might have been slightly behind the United States, but not by much. China was the more aggressive central bank, with its money supply reaching 30% Y-O-Y growth. After that initial spurt, China has been gradually slowing the rate of growth of its money supply.

Europe was different because of the different mandates between the US Fed and the European Central Bank (ECB). Inflation is a severe situation for small countries that have their own currencies,

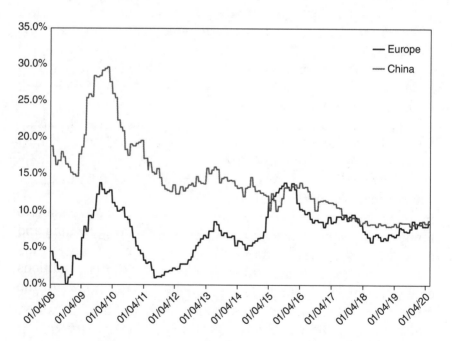

Figure 6.3   Year-Over-Year Money Supply Growth, Europe and China

which was typical in Europe before the European Economic Union. With inflation, a small country's currency gets devalued and the country becomes poorer. The ECB, with only a single mandate, cares only about fighting inflation, not promoting employment or growth. We can only imagine that when they got their money supply growing at 14.5% Y-O-Y in 2009, there must have been extreme discomfort and fist pounding over concern of stimulating the dreaded inflation. Apparently that group prevailed, and they slowed the growth of their money supply to almost zero. With the resulting no inflation and sluggish economic conditions, the ECB once again stimulated growth in the money supply, but grudgingly. During this recovery Europe was a drag on global growth. We believe it contributed to the erratic recovery in the United States. Europe behaved like unified fiefdoms so concerned about inflation that it could not fulfill its role as an economic power.

Peak Conditions

For many years it seemed like there was a contest among observers to see who could be the first to call an end to the multiyear bull market. Of course, they were early and wrong. Watching them be consistently wrong prompted us to look into stock market peaks to see if they had some commonality.

It appears to us that the Fed is the culprit. Seeing a heated economy and rising inflation the Fed tightens monetary policy, which drives the economy into recession. Perhaps the Fed goes too far by mistake or perhaps the Fed thinks it is worth a recession to fight inflation. In either case investors observe the tightening and sell stocks.

In 2015, we looked back at the stock market peak conditions preceding the last four recessions and their bear markets. At the time, we determined a market peak was not in sight because the conditions of rapid economic growth and inflation that would prompt the Fed to tighten were not occurring.

Is There a Market Peak and Subsequent Bear Market in Sight?

April 1, 2015

In early March 2015, the stock market advance had its sixth birthday. How much longer it can go before it hits a peak is anyone's guess. Let's define a peak and see what peaks look like so we will know if one is approaching. There have been four market peaks that preceded bear markets since 1980. Figure 6.4 shows the beginning and ending dates for those bear markets and the negative rates of returns for the S&P 500 Index.

It is important to note that we have excluded from this list the market declines that we call "volatility events," such as the reaction to the invasion of Kuwait (1990), the Asian Contagion (1998), and the two European debt crises (2010

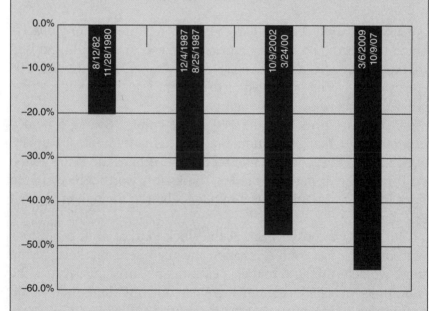

Figure 6.4   Bear Markets

and 2011). We believe those volatility events are unpredictable, short-term reactions to specific events during bull markets that didn't lead to any long-term market decline.

We believe these peaks have some commonality: above average economic growth and developing inflationary pressures. Trailing four-quarter nominal GDP growth was in the 6% to 7% range in the quarters surrounding each of the previous four market peaks mentioned. Further, year-over-year increases in CPI were in the 5.5% to 6.2% range in the quarters immediately preceding and following these four peaks. Contributing to the CPI increases were shortages, and accompanying price increases, in certain goods such as oil in 1980 and building products in 2007. The Federal Reserve has two objectives: full employment and price stability. Responding to the CPI increases and pursuing its objective of price stability preceding each of these market peaks, the Fed drained reserves to slow the growth of the money supply and slow down the economy. Each time, the stock market peaked and then declined.

Table 6.1 shows the year-over-year increase in both CPI and nominal GDP for two (−2Q) and one (−1Q) quarters before the stock market peak as well as for the quarter of the market peak (Peak Q) and the quarter immediately following the peak (+1Q). For example, for the market peak of 11/28/1980 (fourth quarter 1980), the data are from 6/30/80 (−2Q), 9/30/80 (−1Q), 12/31/80 (Peak Q), and 3/31/81 (+1Q).

Is our economy anywhere near the levels that would prompt the Fed to slow the economy to fight inflation? Table 6.2 shows the same CPI and GDP data for the third and fourth quarters 2014, the first quarter 2015, and forecasts for second quarter 2015.

(continued)

(continued)

Table 6.1 GDP & CPI Around Market Peaks

Peak	Data	Quarter Surrounding			
		-2Q	-1Q	Peak Q	+1Q
11/28/80	CPI	14.4%	12.6%	12.5%	10.5%
	GDP	8.0%	7.1%	9.6%	12.0%
8/25/87	CPI	3.0%	3.7%	4.4%	4.4%
	GDP	4.8%	5.7%	6.0%	7.5%
3/24/00	CPI	14.4%	12.6%	12.5%	10.5%
	GDP	8.0%	7.1%	9.6%	12.0%
10/9/07	CPI	14.4%	12.6%	12.5%	10.5%
	GDP	8.0%	7.1%	9.6%	12.0%
		Previous Four Market Peaks			
Average	CPI	3.4%	3.4%	4.5%	5.0%
	GDP	2.8%	3.1%	3.1%	3.8%

Table 6.2 Current Conditions: April 1, 2015

	3Q '14	4Q '14	1Q '15	2Q '15
CPI	1.7%	0.8%	0.0%	–0.1%
GDP	4.3%	3.7%	2.2%	3.0%

As can be seen, CPI is nowhere near the levels of the previous market peaks and, it would seem to us, not near levels that would prompt the Fed to attempt to reduce it. Trailing one-year GDP is modest and, apart from 2007, below levels seen at previous market peaks when the Fed attempted to slow it down.

Because we believe the late 1970s and early 1980s were unusual in terms of inflation, Table 6.3 recomputes the averages for the remaining three peaks discussed. We believe the

Table 6.3 Previous Three Peaks

	-2Q	-1Q	Peak Q	+1Q
CPI	2.8%	3.1%	4.1%	4.0%
GDP	5.2%	5.7%	5.6%	6.1%

data still lend support to our belief that as of the first quarter 2015, the conditions that would trigger the Fed to slow the economy to fight inflation are not in place. Notice that the average year-over-year increase in CPI and GDP at each market peak was 4.1% and 5.6%, respectively. For the first quarter of 2015 CPI is at 0% and GDP is only 2.2%.

We expect it will be at least two years, and perhaps four years, before the inflation and growth conditions would suggest to the Fed the need to tighten monetary policy and slow the economy to fight inflation. Accordingly, we do not expect the conditions surrounding market peaks to form for two to four years. Supporting our optimism for stock prices is our valuation methodology. The average value-to-price (V/P) ratio for all the domestic stocks in the ICON database has been in the 1.07 to 1.08 range in late March 2015, meaning stocks, on average, are still priced below our estimate of fair value. At a market peak, we would expect over pricing (V/P below 1.00) driven by investor optimism and confidence.

We expect the market advance can last at least a couple of more years.

That paper was distributed April 1, 2015, and proved to be correct. Although many observers were calling for an end to the bull market, peak conditions were just not in sight.

Neutral Monetary Policy

From 1926 through 1981, before the multi-decade run of disinflation and declining interest rates, the average yield on Treasury Bills equaled inflation, a very sensible relationship. T-Bills are backed by the full faith and credit of the US Government and are therefore considered to be risk free. You know exactly what your return will be, which means no risk or uncertainty. An investor who does not take risk should not gain on inflation but should just hold even. So, it was very sensible that over many decades the average yield on T-Bills equaled the inflation rate.

Applying this risk-return relationship, when the yield on T-Bills equals the inflation rate, we would label monetary policy as neutral, neither tight nor easy. In that setting, risk-free investors are holding even with inflation. During fall 2018, inflation was being measured in the 2% range, yet the Fed raised its Federal Funds target to near 2.50% and T-Bills fell in line. As the Fed was hinting at more rate increases in 2019, investors sold stocks and headed for the exits during fall 2018. The Fed had been saying it was "data driven" but instead was hinting that it was predetermined to take Federal Funds to 3% or greater in 2019. Just because of historic average or what the Fed might have thought was normal, there was no need to take T-Bills to 3% or more when we were in a low inflation environment. Fortunately, the Fed backed off and stated the Federal Funds target rate would remain constant in 2019. July 2019, the Fed lowered the Federal Funds target range to 2.00% to 2.25%, still a bit above inflation but closer to neutral. With two more rate cuts in September and October it finally returned to a neutral policy with T-Bill just about in line with inflation.

M1 Not Rates

This bull market was so unloved that we saw many analysts skip over it and worry about the next recession. They reasoned that with interest rates so low, reducing the Federal Funds rate would not stimulate the economy. They suggested the Fed would be powerless during the next recession. For example, from the *Wall Street Journal* on December 9, 2019, an article titled "Fed's Tools for Bad Times Grow Dull" states, "It isn't news that the Federal Reserve has less room to counteract a recession by cutting its benchmark interest. In the past three down turns, the central bank has cut rates by at least 5 percentage points. The Fed couldn't do that now because the rate is in a range between 1.50% and 1.75% and unlikely to rise soon."

About a month later, there was a similar line of reasoning expressed in *Bloomberg News* from the article titled "Fed Officials Subtly Shift Inflation Strategy Amid Review" on January 28, 2020, by Christopher Condon. "Yet there is a dark side to low inflation, one that could prove painful if the economy takes a sharp downturn. Low inflation and low growth together mean interest rates are also low, and that robs the Fed of ammunition it may need to fight off a recession. At the moment, the Fed's benchmark rate sits close to 1.5%. Since World War II the Fed has reacted to recessions by lowering rates, on average, by about 5 percentage points. In other words, the Fed is likely to hit zero before it can provide sufficient fuel for a rebound."

Built into that reasoning is the popular belief that it is the level of interest rates that affects the economy. Simply stated, raising the Federal Funds rate slows the economy and lowering the rate stimulates the economy. That line of reasoning is popular because when the Fed performs monetary policy all observers see is the interest rate change, and the one-on-one relationship between rates and the economy is intuitive.

We disagree and believe it is the resulting change in the rate of growth of the money supply, not the change in the Federal Funds rate that affects the economy. Even with low interest rates the Fed has three tools that can be effective to increase the money supply and stimulate the economy. Two inject reserves into banks and all three allow banks to make more loans, which grows M1. First, the Fed can lower the Fed Funds target and perform Open Market Operations. It buys T-Bills from banks and pays for them by adding to the bank's reserves. Then banks can make more loans. Second, the Fed can lower the rate on the Discount Window. Day-to-day, banks borrow reserves from each other, which does not increase reserves over the entire banking system, but when the Fed lowers the rate at the Discount Window, banks borrow reserves from the Fed, which injects reserves into the system. Again, more reserves means more loans because there is a fixed ratio of loans per dollar of reserves on each bank's balance sheet. Third, the Fed can lower the Reserve Requirement. Immediately banks can put more loans on the books per dollar of reserves that they hold. All three tools result in more loans, which creates money; more money, M1, more economic growth. It isn't the change in interest rates that promotes growth, it is the increase in the money supply, and the Fed has the ability to do that even in a low interest rate environment. We saw that in 2020, to be covered in a later chapter.

Summary

The Fed attempted to ease and stimulate monetary and economic growth in August 2007 but the banking system was frozen. With banks unable to make loans, the money supply didn't grow for almost an extra year and a half, which made the recession very severe. Finally, by early 2009, banks made loans, the money supply grew, and the economy recovered. Rather than keeping its foot on the monetary gas pedal, the Fed backed off, presumably due to inflation concerns, only to stimulate again a year later. In addition, the ECB also backed off its stimulative monetary policy, so Europe became a drag on global growth. China was on a path of slower monetary growth. The result of monetary policies in the United States, Europe, and China was an imperfect economic recovery in the United States of two steps forward, one step back, which invited occasional predictions of a double-dip recession. Such an economic setting did not serve as an invitation for investors to buy stocks. On the contrary, it kept investors away.

Can we grade the Fed for its behavior during the recession and bull market? Some feared it eased too much and would cause inflation. They were wrong, so their grade doesn't count. On the contrary, the only fault we find is that the Fed was overly concerned about inflation early in the bull market and backed off its monetary stimulus before the economy could move from recovery to expansion. Then again in 2018, fearing the imaginary inflation monster it raised the Federal Funds rate and drained reserves. So, how about a B? And by the way, the government doesn't print (create) money (M1).

- Initial (2007) monetary ease didn't work because the banking system was frozen.
- After unlocking the banking system money supply grew, stocks rallied, and the economy recovered.
- Fed and ECB feared inflation and quit easing too soon.
- Inflation and GDP were not heated enough to require tightening.
- It's M1 not interest rates.

Chapter 7
Unemployment

One of the biggest concerns that kept investors on the sidelines, missing the bull market, was that they did not think unemployment was improving fast enough. Stock market television focused in on every Friday's release of the jobs report as though it was extremely important for investing. Here is an example in the *Wall Street Journal* on June 30, 2010. Kevin Mahn, portfolio manager at Hennion & Walsh's SmartGrowth Funds, said the ADP report didn't bode well for the government's report or for consumer spending. "With an unemployment rate near 10% . . . we're not going to see consumers spending when they're out of work or worried about their job situation. That's where my concern lies and that's where consumer confidence is now starting to read that as well."

The concern about unemployment was based on the belief that consumer spending was a function of employment. Some economist reasoned that if unemployment didn't drop quickly, the consumer would not spend.

Believing the focus on unemployment was wrong and contributing to investors missing out on the bull market we wrote a report in July 2010 titled "Unemployment Statistics Don't Tell You How to Invest."

Unemployment Statistics Don't Tell You How to Invest

July 16, 2010

It seems unemployment is the number one concern for investors who ponder the economy. They worry that jobs are not being created and, therefore, do not find the stock market attractive. The following data will show that they are worried about something that really doesn't matter.

During the 2008–2009 recession the unemployment rate hit a high of 10.1%. The closest comparison is the recession of 1982, when that rate was a bit worse at 10.8%. Figure 7.1 lines up the peak months for the two recessions. It can be seen that before entering the recession in 1982 the unemployment rate was much higher than what it was preceding the 2008–2009 recession. In the early 1980s the rate

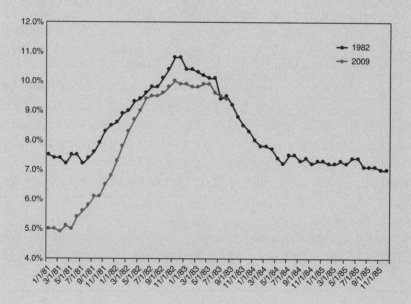

Figure 7.1 Unemployment Rate, 1982 and 2008 Recession

was over 7%, whereas in 2007 the rate was in the 5% range. Second, the post-peak reduction rate is very similar to what it was back in 1983. Third, it is clear that as the economy recovered from the 1982 recession the unemployment rate remained high for many years, taking 14 months just to get down to 8% and staying at 7% or above for another two years.

Despite this sluggish improvement in unemployment, the stock market delivered great returns off that recession's low of August 12, 1982. Table 7.1 shows returns for the S&P 500 Index for the one-, two-, three-, four-, and five-year periods off that low. Furthermore, the one-year period off the most recent recession's March 9, 2009, low is also shown.

Of course we don't know whether the two-, three-, four-, or five-year numbers off the March 9, 2009, low will be as impressive as the numbers off the August 12, 1982, low, but we believe this table suggests stock prices and investors were focused on other fundamentals in 1982, not unemployment. For example, corporate earnings may have been more important to investors than unemployment statistics. As reported, EPS for the S&P 500 companies grew the next two years off the low in 1982, as presented in Table 7.2. The table also reflects estimates for 2010 and 2011.

Table 7.1 S&P 500 Index Returns Off Recession Lows

Range	8/21/82 (%)	3/9/09 (%)
1 Year	66.1	72.3
2 Years	77.4	?
3 Years	110.3	?
4 Years	183.1	?
5 Years	299.1	?

(continued)

(continued)

Table 7.2 S&P 500 Earnings Per Share (EPS)
Year-Over-Year Percentage Change

1982–1983	11.0%	2009–2010 (Estimated)	29.7%
1983–1984	18.6%	2009–2010 (Estimated)	14.3%

Although employment numbers were slow to improve in the early 1980s, they did not seem to dramatically hinder earnings data and the stock market. We don't believe unemployment should or will have a deleterious effect on earnings or the market this time either. Unemployment data may be material to employers hiring or workers looking for jobs. And the issue may even be useful to politicians trying to unseat opponents or talk show hosts trying to increase ratings. Based on what we've seen in the past, however, unemployment data have never been useful for investing.

Figure 7.2 is an updated version of the graph shown in the 2010 paper through the end of 1989 and 2016 for the two recessions. During the first four years of recovery, unemployment improved a bit faster in the 1980s. Then, for the next year and a half, unemployment was about the same for each time period. After five and a half years into recovery, unemployment dropped below 5% for the recent expansion, whereas that level proved to be a barrier in the 1980s. In either case investors weren't buying unemployment. They were buying stocks and stock prices were moving higher. Based on the relationship between unemployment and stock prices the last time unemployment was greater than 10% (1981) we had a road map for stock prices following 2009.

In the 2010 paper we showed a table of returns for the S&P 500 Index for one, two, three, four, and five years out after the bottom in 1982 and hinted that with similar unemployment

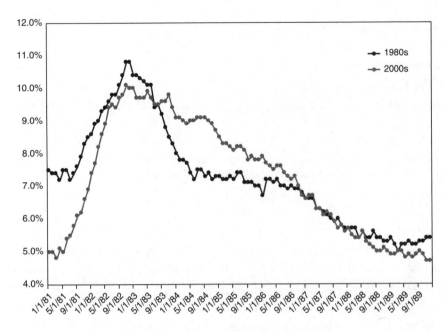

Figure 7.2   Unemployment Rate, 1982 and 2008 Recessions

situations, the 2009 recovery stock market could follow a similar path. Table 7.3 is an updated version, and indeed the market marched higher both times while many investors worried needlessly about unemployment.

Table 7.3   S&P 500 Returns Off Two Market Bottoms

	8/21/82 (%)	3/9/09 (%)
1 Year	66.1	72.3
2 Years	77.4	103.4
3 Years	110.3	115.8
4 Years	183.1	149.7
5 Years	299.1	208.8
6 Years	227.0	248.9
7 Years	344.9	241.1
8 Years	347.8	314.2
9 Years	436.2	397.7
10 Years	495.0	399.7
11 Years	558.0	410.2

Spending Leads Employment

The primary premise behind the concern about unemployment was the belief that employment was the key to consumer spending, as seen in the quote in the opening paragraph of this chapter. In other words, many investors believed that jobs caused (lead to) spending; jobs go up, spending follows and goes up. Jobs go down, spending follows and goes down. For many investors the relationship of jobs causing spending had intuitive appeal. Unfortunately, it was wrong, so their reasoning was misguided.

We have examined personal consumption, nondurables, and unemployment back to 1966 and found no relationship to where unemployment leads spending. We just cannot find any empirical support for the notion that changes in jobs cause changes in spending. Just the opposite: we find slight support for the notion that spending leads or causes jobs. The last recession shows an example of spending leading jobs. Figure 7.3 shows personal consumption

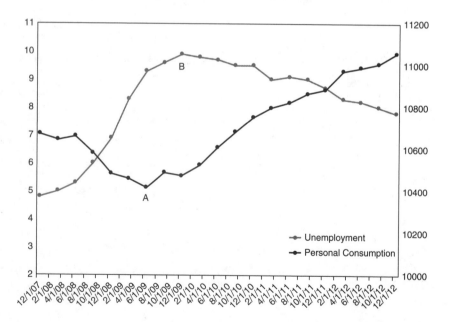

Figure 7.3 Personal Consumption and Unemployment, 12/31/07–12/31/12

and unemployment during the last recession. Personal consumption hit its low June 30, 2009, point A. Unemployment hit its high six months later, December 31, 2009, point B. People started spending more, then six months later jobs increased (unemployment dropped). Jobs followed spending; spending didn't follow jobs.

In the 2020 recession, personal consumption and unemployment turned together. Personal consumption did not lead as in 2009, but again there was no relationship to where unemployment improved and then personal consumption followed. That is consistent with the concept that employment data are not predictors of future consumption behavior.

Unfortunately, many investors didn't fully participate in the great bull market because they thought unemployment was remaining too high. They reasoned that with stubbornly high unemployment, consumer spending would dwindle, but their concerns were misguided because there is no leading relationship between unemployment and consumer spending.

Phillips Curve

When unemployment did get down to the 5% range, inflation fears emerged, because some investors thought there might be upward pressure on wages. Here is a report we wrote in 2015 making the case that we could have low unemployment and low inflation.

Relax—We Are on a Good Phillips Curve

April 27, 2015

The Phillips curve (the curve), first presented in 1958 by A.W.H. Phillips, represents the available trade-off between inflation and unemployment at any point in time.

(continued)

(continued)

The hypothetical Phillips curve in Figure 7.4 is a demonstration of this trade-off whereby attempts to reduce inflation by slowing the economy would cause unemployment to rise. Or, inversely, stimulating the economy to decrease unemployment could cause inflation to increase. Notice, however, the trade-off is not constant, as the line is not straight. For example, at point A, a reduction in inflation could be accomplished with a minimal increase in unemployment, but at point B, a slight reduction in inflation would be very costly in terms of unemployment.

When originally presented, it was hoped that the Phillips curve would persist for very long periods (decades). However, debate in the 1970s proved convincing that any one curve exists for only a short time period (a few years). In other words, the trade-off between inflation and

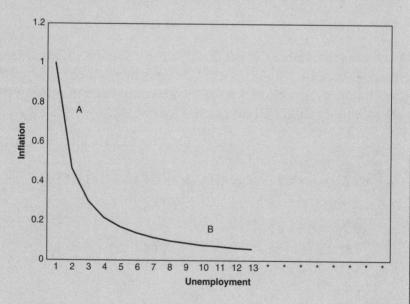

Figure 7.4   Hypothetical Phillips Curve

unemployment may exist in the short term but has not been observed over long periods. We believe that, at any point in time, the position and shape of the curve is determined by numerous factors such as resources (land, labor, and capital) and demand for goods and services, which are functions of demographics. The mobility of resources is a foundation of the free-market system and while we have infringed on that mobility through protectionism in some industries, labor unions, subsidies, and tariffs to name just a few, resources do change over time. Thus, ICON believes that the curve and its trade-off between inflation and unemployment exists in the short run, while its shape and position move around over time as resources and demands change.

For a few years in the late 1970s, during a time labeled "stagflation" by economists, unemployment was in the 6% to 8% range with inflation in the 5% to 13% range. The resources and demands at the time dictated a very unpleasant Phillips curve. Now, however, thirty-five years later with an entirely different mix of land, labor, and capital, and different demands for goods and services, we believe the economy faces a much friendlier set of inflation and unemployment combinations. In other words, we believe we are sitting on a very pleasant Phillips curve.

Obviously, one does not need to know what a Phillips curve is to be a successful stock and bond investor, but we think it does explain, at least in part, a lot of what has happened during the stock market advance of the last six years. Along the way, some analysts feared an accommodative monetary policy by the Federal Reserve would cause increased inflation, but it hasn't. Some argued inflation and other factors would cause interest rates to rise, but interest rates have not risen. During the two "European Debt Crises,"

(continued)

(continued)

there were predictions of a double-dip recession with the usual rise in unemployment, but that didn't happen. Many forecast that unemployment would not come down during the economic recovery, but so far it has, a trend we expect to continue. We believe we are in a docile, forgiving economic setting, and the current blend of land, labor, and capital and demand for goods and services puts us on a friendly Phillips curve.

Gradually declining unemployment and low inflation have been a nice setting for the stock market advance of the last six years. We do not think any politicians contributed to that setting; it is simply that our mix of resources, demands, and demographics have put us on a very nice Phillips curve. We think these conditions can continue for a while.

The case for low unemployment and low inflation coexisting made in that report in 2015 proved correct. Unemployment continued to decline from 5.4% in April 2015 to 3.5% in February 2020. Inflation remained low and stock indexes climbed to all-time highs in 2018, 2019, and early 2020.

Summary

Early in the bull market some investors didn't think unemployment was dropping or improving quickly enough. Then later in the bull market they worried that low unemployment would cause inflation. Both fears proved wrong and probably kept some investors from participating in the bull market. Requiring greatly improving unemployment as a necessary condition for investing in stocks did not prove productive. For one, employment does not lead spending. Two, improvement in unemployment was just as sluggish following the 1981 recession and the stock market rallied nicely back then. Low unemployment and low inflation could coexist because we were on a very good Phillips curve.

- Unemployment is one of the biggest concerns among investors.
- Following the recessions of 1982 and 2009, the stock market rallied despite sluggish improvement in unemployment.
- There is no leading relationship between jobs and spending.
- Being on a friendly Phillips Curve, low inflation and low unemployment can coexist.

Chapter 8

Betting on a Lackluster Stock Market and Higher Interest Rates

I nvestors who did not recognize that the stock market was in a multiyear bull market and didn't fully participate simply lost an opportunity to increase their wealth. Their actions didn't hurt anybody else, just themselves. Investors who expected interest rates to increase missed an opportunity to earn high returns in stocks and bonds, but their inaction didn't hurt anybody else. There is, however, an institutional example in which the belief that the bull market was not for real and the belief that interest rates would rise combined to cause a disaster and hurt a lot of people. First, some background.

You may have noticed on investment advertising the disclosure "Past returns are no guarantee of future results." That warning is a standard requirement for advertisements, but there is a group that doesn't believe it. They believe past returns are predictive of future returns. They are called *actuaries* and they usually have an office in the basement of an insurance company. Based on historic returns, actuaries believe they know the probabilities for returns for any future period such as five, ten, or twenty years. They and the insurance companies they work for count on the stock market repeating itself. Insurance companies take in premiums for policies, promise or guarantee a modest return to the policyholder, and invest a portion of the premiums in the stock market for its higher returns. The insurance company keeps the difference between the higher return it earns in the stock market and the modest, lower return it pays the policyholder.

With variable annuities, the policyholders can put their money into equity mutual funds within an insurance policy and participate in the return of the stock market. The insurance company usually offers some guaranteed income stream in the future. Of course, the actuaries and the insurance companies are counting on the stock and bond market delivering historic returns and are even hedging to insure it—except in one case.

In 2010, an insurance company in Ohio deviated from rigidly believing past returns would be predictive of future returns and brought out an annuity based on the dual beliefs the bull market was not sustainable and interest rates would increase. Both were wrong as we look back and aligned with the views of the common person on the street. The insurance company brought out its "Managed Volatility" variable annuity, with equity funds that did not have the objective of maximizing returns, but the objective of reducing volatility. Of course, returns are sacrificed to accomplish reduced volatility and the funds did not fully participate in the bull market. Yet, the annuities promised very impressive income streams out in the future. We can only presume that behind the scenes, the insurance company executives reasoned that they didn't need historic stock market returns to accumulate a lot of assets to generate adequate yields because interest rates would be much higher when the policy annuitized.

Think of how easy these policies were to sell. Investors didn't believe in the bull market and were still looking in their rearview mirrors at 2008 and early 2009. Reduced volatility was very appealing as was the impressive guaranteed income in the future. But, the bull market charged on and interest rates dropped. The insurance company executives should have listened to the actuaries and not overruled them with personal views of the stock market and interest rates. The equity funds did not accumulate enough assets to generate the promised income, especially at the lower interest rates. First, a little background before telling what happened.

ICON had managed three mutual funds inside that company's variable annuity since 2004. In 2010, they approached us and asked us, in a sense, to merge our balanced fund and our covered call fund together specifically for the Managed Volatility platform. The fund was then called Risk Managed Balanced and was a balanced fund (stocks and bonds) with options used to dampen the volatility of stocks. For many years it was the number one or number two performing fund on the platform and eventually got put into their model portfolio. On July 31, 2012, ICON presented to the variable annuity's mutual fund board of trustees. On one slide we showed that the stock market had gained 100.6% in 157 weeks off the March 9, 2009, low. We stated the market advance could continue at least a few more years and that "markets like this just don't come around very often." We declared that in a market like this it is silly to invest to reduce volatility and that you should just "try to make as much money as you can." With their view that the bull market was not for real, they probably dismissed our view just like they did the actuaries' opinion.

Unable to deliver on their promised level of income, the insurance company called a phone meeting of their variable annuity sales staff and fired all of them in September 2018. They said they were stopping sales on variable annuities and stopping payments of trail commissions to financial advisors. They also held a call for managers of funds within the variable annuity. They explained what they were doing and most managers were silent, but ICON asked the question, "Do you have a plan for retaining assets?" The simple answer was, "No!" Then it hit us, unable to honor the income promised, they were hoping accounts would close and go away.

Financial advisors have tried suing the insurance company for defaulting on paying the trail commissions but so far have not been successful. Courts have ruled that the selling agreement was between the insurance company and the broker/dealer, not the advisor. Financial advisors may be barking up the wrong tree.

At the time, the insurance company was a mutual company, meaning it did not have shareholders like a typical corporation. In mutual companies, it is reasoned that the policyholders are the shareholders. The mutual structure is not unique to insurance. Many savings and loans and credit unions are mutual, where the depositors are the shareholders. Policyholders and depositors are very docile. They only care if the policy or deposit is being honored. They don't care about diversity in management, social issues, or how many jets the company owns. They vote for the board of directors by usually just reelecting the existing one. Here is the opening for the financial advisors and anyone else who felt hurt by the shutdown of the variable annuity.

People just don't buy insurance policies and variable annuities through unsolicited calls to the company. They are sold those policies by agents and financial advisors. These agents and advisors could have united and instructed their investors to nominate and elect a new slate of directors. As the old saying goes, "throw the bums out." Then, that new board could have run the company the way they wanted, perhaps reinstating trail commissions.

Disbelief and denial in the bull market and the expectation for rising interest rates were powerful and gut level. They just felt right to many investors and executives, but they were wrong and in this case acting on them caused some damage.

Chapter 9
Volatility Events

We have given the name *volatility event* to a certain situation in the stock market. Stock prices drop about 16% to 20% over about twelve weeks, then recover and resume the long-term upward path they were on before the volatility event. During the descent and especially at the bottom, there is a specific concern that is very well known by investors. In fact, they are focused on it. This is different than the beginning of a bear market when investors are usually baffled by the stock price declines because there is no obvious cause. Volatility events are triggered by news, whereas bear markets begin for no apparent reason. We believe volatility events are unpredictable. They have occurred in 1990, 1998, 2010, 2011, and 2018. Notice there were three of them during the post-2009 bull market. These are agonizing and painful for investors. Having three of them in one multiyear bull market sure contributed to the "unloved" nature. We suspect many investors sold during them and never returned.

Figure 9.1 shows the S&P 500 Index a few months before and a few years after the volatility event of 1990. When Iraq invaded Kuwait, it caught investors by surprise and sent the market into a twelve-week tailspin. There was a sharp decline, an almost equally fast recovery, and then a resumption of the long-term trend. The straight line emphasizes how the sharp drop was just an unpleasant

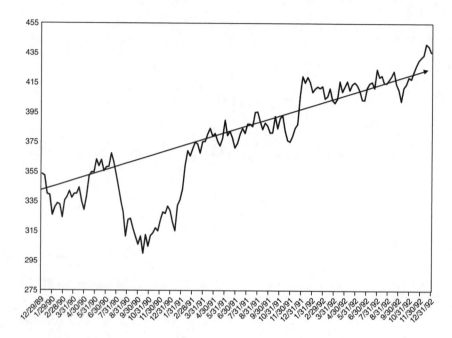

Figure 9.1　　S&P 500 Index, 12/31/1989–12/31/1992

interruption in the long-term trend. At the bottom of all volatility events, it seems like there is no way out. It is difficult for an intelligent, logical person to come up with any scenario for recovery. The negative news just builds and creates a setting of no hope, yet the market rebounds.

1990 and 1998

The sharp drop in 1990 was ignited by the invasion of Kuwait. In 1998, the fear came from what the media called the "Asian Contagion." There was the theory that the recession in Asia would spread to Europe and then spread to the United States. Although later proven to be incorrect, that line of reasoning became very convincing and apparently believed by enough investors to cause a 19.2%

drop in the S&P 500 Index. There were different fears at different times, but volatility events are quite similar. Figure 9.2 shows the S&P 500 Index adjusted to a beginning value of 1.00 for 1990 and 1998. They are similar in depth and duration, although 1998 had a bit faster recovery. Similar to 1990, the market resumed its climb higher in 1998, not peaking until March 2000.

Why show 1990 and 1998? Because it is a pattern and repeated itself three times during the recent multiyear bull market. In 2010 and 2011, investors focused on the European debt crisis with potential defaults on sovereign debt. The drops were not as deep as in the 1990s—15.6% in 2010 and 18.4% in 2011—but the news was equally scary and the outlook just as bleak as at those bottoms. In Figure 9.3, the drops, the duration, and the recoveries in 2010 and 2011 were quite similar. In other words, having lived through events in the 1990s, we had a road map for the volatility events of 2010 and 2011.

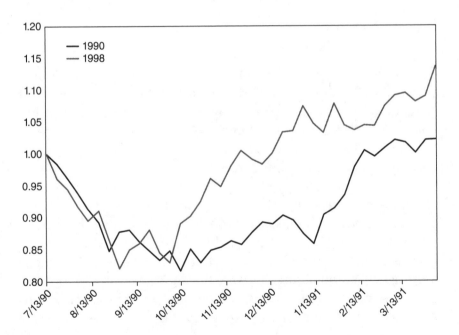

Figure 9.2   1990 and 1998 Volatility Events

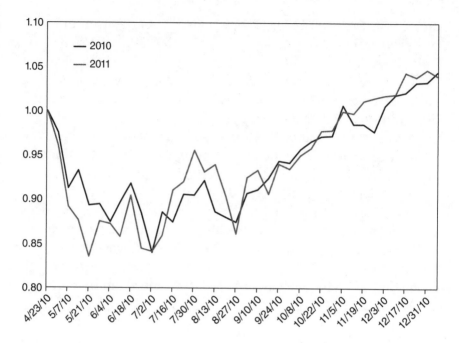

Figure 9.3   S&P 500 Index, 2010 and 2011 Volatility Events

Although the trade war with China was a concern for investors in late 2018, the biggest problem was the belief that the Fed was not "data driven," as it had been saying, but instead predetermined to continue raising the Federal Funds target to well over 3% in 2019. The drop in late 2018 and the rebound most closely resembles the event in 1990 as shown in Figure 9.4.

Although the strategy of buy and hold was very productive for eleven years, it certainly was made difficult by three volatility events. In addition, those events caused problems for most money managers. As shown in Chapter 2 they included complete theme reversals. Over the long run, information technology, consumer discretionary, financials, and industrials were the top-performing sectors, but they suffered the most during the short-term, severe setbacks. Managers generally do not have the ability to "time" twelve-week sector

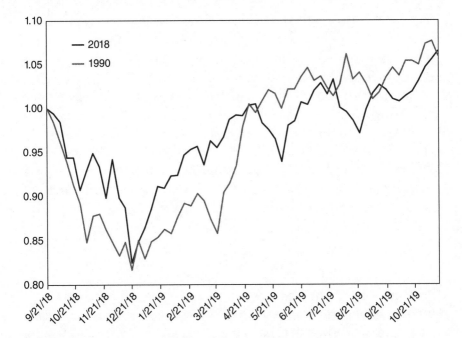

Figure 9.4   S&P 500 Index, 2018 and 1990 Volatility Events

and industry theme reversals. Whether using value, momentum, or most other strategies used by investors and managers, short-term theme reversals prove difficult to handle, especially when they are caused by fears that later on prove to be invalid, in other words, irrational.

CNBC TV

In December 2018, the market bottom was December 24. I was on CNBC TV December 26 on "The Exchange" hosted by Kelly Evans. I was the first guest at 1:00 Eastern time. That day, Bill Griffith was at the desk with Ms. Evans. He asked, "Craig, what do you think?" My response, "We believe we are in what we call a volatility event like

1990, 1998, 2010, and 2011. In those cases, the market dropped 17% to 20% over about nine to twelve weeks, then the market rebounded and resumed its long-term trend. So we expect the same this time . . . It sure feels like a bottom to us."

The market moved higher and two weeks later, I was on the show again. Kelly Evans asked, "The day after Christmas you told us it feels like a bottom now. What happens next?" I said, "So we would expect to get back to those [all-time] highs we saw in September by late March, early April." It actually took until May; we were off by a few weeks because volatility events are remarkably similar but not exactly alike.

Value

Although downright scary, those volatility events produce excellent buying opportunities. At ICON, we compute intrinsic value for stocks and divide by price. Each stock has a value/price (V/P) ratio. Anything above 1.00 means the stock is priced below our estimate of fair value. We take an average of all the stocks in our database to get what we call a market V/P. Table 9.1 shows our market V/P and the discounts to fair value, on average, for stocks at the bottom of the five volatility events. As you'd expect, bad news and attractive bargains go hand-in-hand. You don't get discounts that attractive because the news is good. Good discounts go with bad news and bleak outlooks.

Table 9.1   Market V/P

Year	Market V/P
1990	1.20
1998	1.35
2010	1.34
2011	1.52
2018	1.15

Setbacks and Theme Reversals

Although the volatility events of 2010, 2011, and 2018 were the biggest drops, there were five other noteworthy setbacks. We have divided the eleven-year bull market into nine advances and eight declines based on short-term troughs and peaks. The longest advance was 102 weeks from February 2016 to January 2018. The shortest was fifteen weeks June to September 2014. The average advance was fifty weeks. The longest drop was thirty-eight weeks from May 2015 to February 2016 and the shortest was just six weeks from September to October 2014. The average decline lasted 15 weeks. Table 9.2 shows sector rates of return ranked by "up-market" performance and reveals extreme theme reversals.

In Chapter 2 we saw that over the entire bull market information technology, consumer discretionary, financials, and industrials were the four best-performing sectors. Here we see that they were the leaders during the phases when the market advanced, but we also see how they got hit during the down phases. The long-term lagging and so-called recession-proof sectors, such as consumer staples, utilities, and telecommunication services, were sluggish when the market advanced but held up the best during down phases.

Table 9.2 Sector Returns in Up and Down Phases

	Up (%)	Down (%)
Financials	48.5	–14.9
Information Technology	48.3	–13.0
Consumer Discretionary	45.4	–12.0
Industrials	42.8	–13.8
Materials	40.4	–16.5
S&P 1500 Index	37.6	–12.2
Health Care	32.5	–9.3
Energy	28.8	–19.5
Consumer Staples	22.4	–5.3
Utilities	18.2	–1.5
Telecommunication Services	17.6	–5.5

With the average advance being just fifty weeks and the average drop being just fifteen weeks, these are extremely rapid theme reversals that are very difficult on active managers. Most managers do not have the ability to "time" fifteen-week-long sector themes.

As a side note, energy was the worst sector over the entire bull market but not because it didn't participate in rising markets. It lagged the market during advances but still participated. Energy got pounded during down phases similar to materials because both sectors have a commodity price sensitivity. Also in 2018, S&P changed telecommunication services into communication services. For this table we use the identity it had for nine of the eleven years.

What contributed to the volatility and short-term theme reversals? Was it jitters? Was it the lack of confidence? Was it the two steps forward, one step back nature of the economic recovery? Was it the on-again, off-again monetary policy of the Fed and the European Central Bank? Whatever it was, these short-term drops and complete theme reversals were unpleasant, scaring investors and creating headaches for money managers.

Accepting the Stock Market as It Is

In fall 2018 we wrote a paper to try to help investors ride through the dips, theme reversals, and volatility of this bull market.

Why Can't the Market Adapt to My Needs?

August 2018

The purpose of this article is to help remind financial advisors and their investors of the power of long-term investing and the potential cost of investor fear.

The S&P 500 Index has averaged 15.93% over the last 9+ years (1/30/09–6/30/18), but we suspect many investors did not fully participate. To help make our points let's look at favorite clothing versus the weather.

If New York residents favored flip-flops, shorts, and a t-shirt, it would be very costly and impractical to constantly go where the weather suits their clothes. Such an endeavor would disrupt personal relationships and mean hopping islands, continents, and hemispheres. The less-expensive and more practical alternative would mean changing clothes to adapt to the changing weather.

Investors can either accept, and adapt to, stock market behavior (changing weather) or try to make the stock market suit them (and their clothes, so to speak). Figure 9.5 is

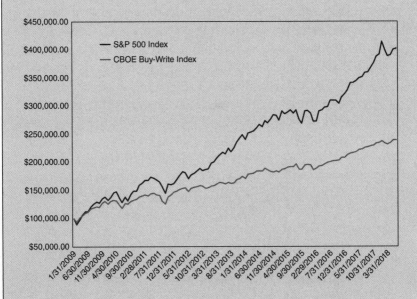

Figure 9.5   Cost of Reducing Volatility

(continued)

(continued)

a graph that shows the S&P 500 more than tripled between January 30, 2009, and June 30, 2018. It is noticeable that there have been some setbacks and volatility along the way. Rather than remain fully invested, in an attempt to reduce volatility and make the market suit them, some investors held cash, attempted short-term market timing, wrote call options, bought put options, sold short, and/or invested in "alternatives." Instead of carefully considering the weather report, then putting on a raincoat, they traveled all over the investment map to find the weather that suited their personal comfort zone.

Just as traveling around the world in order to keep wearing flip-flops is expensive, jumping out of the market to stay "comfortable" can be costly. It is also, we would argue, unnecessary and counterproductive. After all, why do you need an alternative to tripling your money in eight and a half years? We contend the "buy and hold" approach has been more effective than trying to time market peaks and bottoms and haphazardly jumping in and out of the market.

As an example of the potential costs of reducing portfolio volatility, the Chicago Board Option Exchange's S&P 500 BuyWrite Index allows you to track the performance of a hypothetical strategy of holding the S&P 500 Index and writing call options against the equities. Writing options generally sacrifices some upside potential, but the strategy is intended to provide a downside cushion with lower volatility. We would argue that writing options for volatility reduction during a bull market could be interpreted as an effort to make the behavior of the stock market suit the investor's risk tolerance. As seen in Figure 9.5, if someone had invested one hundred thousand dollars in the S&P 500 Index on January 30, 2009, and held through June 30, 2018, that initial investment would have grown into $393,000. By contrast one hundred thousand dollars invested in the buy-write strategy would have grown to only $235,850. In this one example, focused on the market rally, it cost about $157,150 to make the stock market suit the investor's risk tolerance.

If you are investing for retirement, your goal is presumably to accumulate enough wealth to stop working and have enough money to do what you want. For some that might mean buying a home in Florida, Arizona, or another warm climate. For others, it might mean traveling around the world. In any case, the person selling the house or travel package does not take risk-adjusted returns as payment. They take money, and the investor who bought smartly and held the last nine-plus years has been on a wealth accumulation path and may today be in a position to afford that house or trip. We salute them and hope that our bullish analysis and commentary have encouraged them along the way.

Summary

There were three volatility events during the eleven-year bull market, and they were very similar to the previous two in the 1990s. The market dropped sharply over nine to twelve weeks while investors focused on a well-known, obvious concern or situation. The potential recession never happened and in all cases the market bounced back quickly and resumed its pre-volatility event path higher.

Volatility events are good examples of "the market can be wrong." Investors sell, fearing and even predicting some event or situation, then it never happens. Paul Samuelson, noted economist at MIT declared, "The stock market is a leading indicator; it has predicted nine of the last five recessions." The market did that three times during this multiyear unloved bull market. Unloved? Three volatility events in ten years with two coming in the first two years sure made this multiyear bull market anything but fun. Some investors just couldn't get through those. The great Peter Lynch of Fidelity Magellan fame advised, "The key to making money in stocks is not to get scared out of them."

- A volatility event consists of 16% to 20%, nine- to twelve-week drops, quick recovery, and resumption of the long-term trend.
- 1990, 1998, 2011, 2011, and 2018 were very similar volatility events.
- Three drops during the eleven-year bull market scared investors.
- Volatility events feature complete sector theme reversals.
- Riding through volatility is rewarding. It is expensive to reduce volatility.

Chapter 10

Six Pieces of Bad Information

There were six special beliefs that could have caused investors to miss this great bull market. All the way up, investors were told stocks were too expensive based on the price/earnings (P/E) ratio of the S&P 500 Index. Second, in 2010, some investors took the double-dip recession scenario to an extreme and predicted deflation. Third, corporations were buying back shares of their stock, which for some reason was viewed with suspicion. Bearish investors believed the buybacks were the primary force driving stock prices higher and reasoned, if they quit, look out! Fourth, some observers dismissed the earnings growth because they were disappointed with slow revenue growth. Fifth, by 2016 investors feared that corporations had excessive amounts of debt, which could lead to bankruptcies. Finally, in 2019, an inverted yield curve drove many investors to the sidelines in fear of a subsequent recession. Overpriced? Deflation? Corporate buybacks? Inadequate revenue growth? Excessive debt? Inverted yield curve? Looking back, we know investors should have ignored these situations and bought and held stocks. Let's take them one at a time.

Overpriced?

Besides the imperfect economic recovery, which could have persuaded investors to avoid stocks, there was regular commentary on TV, radio, and in print that the market was expensive, or overpriced. Throughout the multiyear market advance, we have seen analysts caution investors with regard to owning stocks. They have cited the P/E ratio for various indexes such as the S&P 500 Index. Their case has been that a lofty P/E, and therefore apparently expensive stock prices, could predict lower stock prices from that time forward. With our ICON valuation readings in disagreement with this cautious commentary, we published a paper in early 2017.

Deficiencies of P/E in Predicting Returns

May 2017

Throughout the nearly eight-year stock market advance from the recession low of March 2009 through the record highs of March 2017, we have seen some analysts caution investors with regard to owning stocks. Some of these analysts cite the price to earnings (P/E) ratio for various indexes such as the S&P 500 Index and try to make the case that a lofty P/E, and therefore apparently expensive stock prices, could predict lower stock prices from that time forward. With many indexes hitting record highs in March 2017, more and more of those cautious warnings have appeared in the media and advisory services. But, not so fast!

While the notion that lower stock prices should follow expensive stock prices and that higher stock prices should follow cheap stock prices is intuitively appealing, it is not supported by statistics, at least not when using P/E as a

Table 10.1 R-Squared for P/E and Returns	
Period	R2
3 Months	0.0121
6 Months	0.0245
9 Months	0.0345
12 Months	0.0415

measure of value. To illustrate this point, we took the end-of-month P/E ratio for the S&P 500 Index for close to fifty years, from January 1967 through November 2016, and computed simple price change rates of return for three, six, nine, and twelve months later for all rolling periods through November 2016. Table 10.1 shows the R-squared (correlation coefficient) for P/E and subsequent returns for the four different time periods.

An R-square of zero means the relationship between P/E and subsequent returns of the S&P 500 is random, or has no relationship. An R-square value of 1 would mean P/E and subsequent returns of the S&P 500 are perfectly correlated. The first thing that stands out from our computations is that with such low correlations close to zero, P/E may not be good at predicting future returns for the S&P 500. While the correlation does increase slightly from three-month periods to twelve-month periods, even at twelve months, about 95.4% of the returns on the S&P 500 are explained by something other than P/E. In other words, P/E only explains 4.56% of the next year's returns.

The scattergram (Figure 10.1) provides a visual of the random relationship between P/E and future returns. P/E for the S&P 500 is on the horizontal axis and subsequent twelve-month price returns are on the vertical axis. Looking at the

(continued)

(continued)

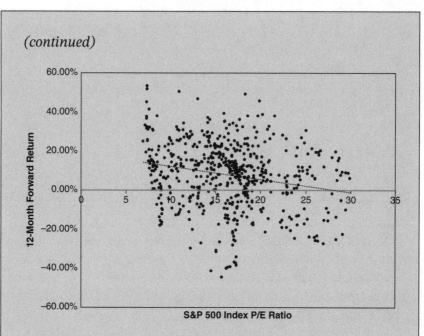

Figure 10.1   S&P 500 Index and Forward Returns

chart, there are plenty of months when the S&P 500 had a low P/E but the return over the next twelve months was negative and/or below average. Also, notice there were plenty of months with high P/E ratios that were followed by above average returns over the next twelve months. The slightly downward sloping line is the linear regression, or best fit, line. The fact that it is downward sloping suggests that what minimal relationship there is between P/E and subsequent twelve-month return is negative. Higher P/Es are associated with slightly lower subsequent returns than lower P/E ratios, but in statistical terms the relationship is extremely weak.

We suspect the slope of the linear regression line is not as steep as those who use P/E to attempt to predict future

Table 10.2 Rate-of-Return, Four P/E Ratios

P/E	Return (%)
10	12.4
15	9.2
20	6.0
25	2.8

returns believe. The regression equation is $Rm = .19 - .0067 \times P/E$, where Rm is the return on the S&P 500 ("the market") and $-.0067$ is the slope coefficient, which is multiplied times the P/E. Table 10.2 computes the expected rate of return for the subsequent year for four different P/E ratios. Over this fifty-year period, a P/E of 10 has been followed by an average return of 12.3%, whereas a P/E of 25 has been followed by an average return of 2.3%.

We suspect that analysts using P/E to recommend selling stocks when the P/E ratio is high would expect the difference between returns following P/E ratios of 10 and 25 to be much greater.

What's wrong? Is it the concept that stocks should be expensive at peaks and cheap at bottom? Or is P/E deficient at measuring value? We submit P/E is deficient. Finance textbooks are uniform in teaching how to calculate the value of any asset—the present value of future cash flows. Cash flows are predicted to grow and then discounted to their present value considering risk and interest rates. Declaring a P/E is too high or too low as a measure of value ignores growth, risk, and interest rates.

At ICON, we compute a value-to-price (V/P) ratio for each stock in our database, which gives us a measure of our estimate of a stock's intrinsic value. To calculate the V/P

(continued)

(continued)

for a company, we start with average earnings and future earnings growth estimates for a company. Then we discount future earnings back to a present value considering risk and a measure of the company's bond yield as the basis for opportunity cost. The average value-to-price (V/P) ratio for all the stocks in the ICON database gives us an indication of the overall under- or overpricing for the broad market according to our system. Based on our research, our overall average market V/P ratio has a steeper slope and higher correlation with future returns than does the simplistic P/E.

In summary, many investors have missed out on some or all of the impressive market advance from its low in March 2009 through record highs in March 2017 because of the belief that stocks were too expensive based on P/E ratios. We believe the concept that stocks are cheap at bottoms and expensive at peaks is valid. P/E is just deficient at measuring value.

A stock price should be a function of four variables: earnings, expected growth in earnings, risk, and an interest rate. As interest rates drop, it is mathematically sensible for P/E to increase, all else being equal. In the low and declining interest rate setting of 2009–2019, it was rational for P/E to increase and be higher than its historic average.

Ignoring the connection between pricing multiples and interest rates isn't new. In the early 1990s we competed against a manager that used price-to-book value to allocate among cash, stocks, and bonds. We can only guess they did their back testing in the 1970s and 1980s with higher interest rates and, therefore, lower price-to-book ratios. By the early 1990s, they thought stocks were too expensive based on a higher than average price-to-book value ratio and held mostly cash. Missing the stock rally of the early 1990s, their performance caused them to lose a lot of assets under management and eventually they went out of business.

Deflation

Over most of this bull market, potential inflation bothered investors as they feared it would result from the expansive monetary policy. In 2010, however, deflation was the headline concern, a byproduct of the double-dip recession fears. Although they didn't like potential deflation alone, they reasoned it would cause many other bad things, such as the inability of borrowers to repay debt. Although we didn't agree and did not expect deflation, we reasoned it wouldn't be all that bad anyway. Here is a paper we wrote for investors in late 2010. We called it "We Do Not Worry About Deflation. Here's Why."

We Do Not Worry About Deflation. Here's Why

August 20, 2010

Spring of 2009, inflation fears spread among investors, causing some to hold cash back from equities. ICON wrote and distributed a paper making the case that inflation should be tame and not a concern in the near future. We were right. Inflation has been tame over the last year. Lately, a new and opposite fear is rapidly circulating the conjecture and rumor circuits. Many market observers are stating that deflation, a decline in prices of goods and services, is possible. They then go on to suggest such a setting is bad for stocks and suggest bonds and some extremely

(continued)

(continued)

defensive investments are better alternatives. They suggest deflation causes certain behaviors and use the threatening word *spiral*. We are skeptical of those claims as we believe deflation is an "affect" of something, not a "cause" of something. In other words, something causes deflation; deflation does not cause anything. Furthermore, if inflation is bad, couldn't deflation be good?

Using Bloomberg, we got the year-over-year change in the Consumer Price Index (CPI) each year going back to 1920. There were eleven years when it was negative showing deflation. Table 10.3 shows those years and the Y-O-Y CPI change and the rate of return on stock market each of those years. Data on the S&P 500 Index only goes back to

Table 10.3 Year-Over-Year CPI Change and Rate-of-Return

Year	CPI (%)	Stocks (%)
1921	–10.80	12.30
1922	–2.30	21.50
1926	–1.10	11.62
1927	–2.30	37.49
1928	–1.20	43.61
1930	–6.40	–24.90
1931	–9.30	–43.34
1932	–10.30	–8.19
1938	–2.80	31.12
1949	–2.10	18.79
1954	–0.70	52.62
Average		13.9%
Excluding Depression		28.63%

1926 so for 1920–1925, the Dow Jones Industrial Average was used. The stock market, as represented by these two indicators, posted losses only three of the eleven years of deflation. Those three years were during the Great Depression: 1930, 1931, and 1932. Over all eleven years of deflation, the average return on stocks was 13.9%. As it would be difficult for anyone predicting deflation to make the case that we are headed for another Great Depression, as conditions now are quite different from 1930, so we can take out the three years of the early 1930s. The remaining eight years the market averaged 28.6%. Just to see if deflation caused something a year later, we looked at just the returns one year following a deflation year and the average return for all eleven years was 14.3%. So there does not appear to be a negative lagging affect.

In summary it does not seem like deflation is something to worry about, at least relative to stock market investing.

As we know now, deflation fears subsided and the market moved higher.

Corporate Buybacks

Public companies can buy back their shares from public investors. They use cash so on the balance sheet cash is reduced and so is total shareholder's equity. The shares show up as treasury stock, which accountants call a *contra account*. These buybacks have to be approved by the board of directors and announced to the public. They usually state a total amount but do not state exactly when they will be buying.

Some analysts view this activity from the negative perspective. They suggest it means the company doesn't have anything better to invest in, such as growth opportunities. They also worry that the buying artificially inflates the stock price and when the repurchasing stops, stock price might revert back to previous levels. Here is an example of a negative view. Craig was on CNBC TV, "The Exchange," on March 1, 2019. After Craig gave his view that the market should go higher, Kelly Evans asked the other guest, Brian Reynolds, "Brian, what about you? How much of a tailwind does this bull market have?" Mr. Reynolds replied, "I think it has a very big tailwind. We had a panic in 2015 and 2016 that launched two years of debt-fueled buybacks, merges, and LBOs. I think we are going to have the same thing: another couple of years of debt-fueled buybacks." The other guest and Craig agreed that the market could move higher. Craig based his on value. The other guest said the move would be supported by "debt-fueled buybacks." Sounds almost sinister and implies the only reason the market is moving higher is because of the "debt-fueled" buybacks.

From the positive side, when you own the stock it is comforting knowing there is a big buyer out there. Some buyback purchases may be in regular intervals; others may wait for dips and add support. Managements and boards are in the best position to see the prospects of the company. Buybacks suggest they like the prospects and think the stock is cheap. Buybacks reduce the number of shares outstanding, which boosts earnings per share when accountants divide earnings by the number of shares outstanding.

By 2010, buybacks were increasing and the voices with the negative view were much louder and more prevalent than those with a positive view. Given the stubbornly high unemployment and fears of double-dip recession at the time, skeptics argued the buybacks falsely inflated stock prices and were the only thing keeping stock prices from dropping. We disagreed and found the buybacks to be a positive signal and addressed it in our October 2010 Portfolio Update, our monthly letter to investors. Here are parts of it.

Portfolio Update

October 5, 2010

In 2010, individual investors are generally selling their positions in equity mutual funds in favor of purchasing bond funds. A *Bloomberg News* article on September 27, 2010, by David Pauly titled "Stock Buybacks Are for Dummies Except Right Now" revealed that many corporations are doing just the opposite. That is, corporations are issuing bonds (at what they perceive to be low interest rates) and using the proceeds to repurchase and retire common stock.

"S&P said it expects buybacks in 2010 to exceed $300 billion, compared with $137,6 billion last year. Many companies borrow at today's low interest rates to finance share repurchases," Bloomberg noted. Individual investors and public corporations are responding very differently to current market conditions. Investors are selling equities and buying bonds while corporations are doing the exact opposite and selling bonds while buying equities. At ICON we believe the corporations are on the correct side of this disconnect, and we view the repurchase activity as positive for the stock market.

The Bloomberg article noted also that buybacks "let firms boost per-share profits by reducing their equity base [that is, the number of shares outstanding] and may indicate executives find their stock undervalued. Evidence that businesses are parting with their record cash shows concern the economy will slip into its second recession in three years is diminishing." An asset manager interviewed for the story commented: "You don't do that [issue debt and buy back shares] unless you feel secure about 2011. It may just be the corporate outlook for 2011 is better than you would gather from economic news."

(continued)

(continued)

We presume corporate executives are basing their buyback decisions on income statements, balance sheets, supply and demand for their products and services, and quantitative valuation models. Individual investors, on the other hand, may be much more influenced by headlines, talk shows, political views, and unpleasant memories of the stock market in 2008 and early 2009. Whatever factors are being evaluated by these two groups, they certainly seem to be very different and lead, in any event, to opposite behaviors. Again, while we have no crystal ball, we believe the decision to sell bonds and buy stocks at this time will be validated over the course of the next two years.

Our ICON market value-to-price (V/P) ratio was in the 1.30 range for much of late September, meaning stock prices, on average, would have to increase 30% just to get to our estimate of fair value. The fact that we see this much value in the current market suggests to us that corporations are acting prudently in taking advantage of this opportunity to buy back cheap shares.

Our analysis of the stock market over the last few decades tells us the market generally experiences themes, with industry leadership that typically lasts one to two years—until now. After surging for six months off the March 9, 2009, low, the broad market has advanced only modestly over the last year, with rapid theme reversals lasting just six to eight weeks. Certain industries have led when the market moved higher, but those same industries declined dramatically when the market turned. The result, in our opinion, has been a "theme-less" trading range with a slight upward drift.

We think individual investors, with their herd-like migration from stocks to bonds, have helped create the current trading environment, the volatility of which has only encouraged them to continue their migration. The cycle goes like this: investors use any market advance as an opportunity to sell equities, which in turn helps grind the advance to a halt. Concurrently, the frustration associated with a choppy market encourages investors to sell more equities. Corporations have been eager to take advantage of this investor uncertainty to buy back their shares.

Summary

Some market observers have used the term *accumulation* to describe market activity immediately preceding market advances. These observers believe stocks are moving from weak hands to strong hands or being "accumulated" by stronger investors—that is, investors who arguably have a better tolerance for this kind of uncertainty. We believe the last several months have been a period of accumulation and that the market will break out to the upside once weak investors have completed their selling. We believe the corporations, which are currently buying back their shares, and the individual investors, who retain their equity positions and ride through this volatility, will be rewarded.

That was back in October 2010. Corporations were issuing bonds and buying their stock. Investors were selling stocks and buying bonds. With two groups with completely opposite behaviors, one side had to be wrong. We thought the corporations would be proven right. They were.

We addressed corporate buybacks in October 2010 from an investment perspective, making a case that the broad market could move higher. The discussion on buybacks continued throughout the multiyear bull market from not only an investment perspective but also from a social view. An article in the December 9,

2019, issue of *Bloomberg Businessweek* by Peter Coy titled "CEOs Goose Their Pay with Buybacks" focused more on the social side and began by stating the magnitude of buybacks. "In 2018, S&P 500 companies bought back a record $806 billion worth of shares, a 55% leap from the year before. They're on track to buy back about $740 billion worth this year." The article then went on to mention two social criticisms. First is that they benefit shareholders but are bad for workers. "This was the line taken by Democratic presidential candidates Elizabeth Warren and Bernie Sanders, who support banning or restricting open-market stock buybacks."

The article then dug into a second, less familiar line of criticism that the buybacks aren't necessarily good for shareholders but benefit corporate executives and directors.

> Leading the charge for this cause is Robert Jackson, a Securities and Exchange commissioner who's been agitating for more than a year for his agency to schedule hearings on the issue. . . Jackson had his staff study 385 recent buybacks. They found that shares rose by about 2.5% more than would otherwise have been expected in the days after a buyback announcement. They found that, compared with an ordinary day, twice as many companies see executives and directors sell shares in the eight days after a buyback announcement. The value of sales goes up too. In the days before a buyback, selling by insiders averages less than $100,000 a day. In the days after a buyback, that average climbs to more than $500,000 a day.

As for insiders and directors, regulations for their buying and selling activity are already established. Adding restrictions on selling into buybacks would be an easy add-on for regulators if Mr. Jackson can successfully present adequate evidence and make his case.

The stock market helps allocate the limited resources of land, labor, and capital for our society as stock prices set the terms for companies to get capital. An efficient allocation of resources promotes low unemployment and low inflation, whereas an inefficient, wasteful allocation does the opposite. As time passes, society's demands for goods and services change due to technology, inventions, demographics, and many other influences. Therefore, the allocation of our limited resources must be fluid. Initial public offerings (IPOs) and buybacks are just part of the ebb and flow of the free market system. Some companies may have needed and obtained capital a few decades ago to produce what society wanted then but now they don't need the capital. They can buy back shares. The investors selling the stock can use the proceeds to invest in a new IPO, a company producing some new good or service that society wants and is willing to pay for. For example, tobacco and coal companies can repurchase their shares while Uber, Facebook, and Netflix go public and receive capital. It seems simple and suggests buybacks perform a function for society in allocating its resources and are nothing to worry about in a bull market.

Lackluster Revenue Growth and Earnings

In Chapter 2, Figure 2.2 showed how earnings per share grew for the S&P 1500 companies during the eleven-year bull market. Yet many skeptical observers with a predetermined bearish mindset dismissed those earnings. They stated that there was lackluster growth in revenue (sales) so the earnings growth was simply due to cost cutting. They would not acknowledge the earnings growth and we presume did not embrace the bull market.

It turns out it is normal for earnings to grow more than revenue. That relationship between revenue and earnings is due to operational and financial leverage, topics covered in a chapter in undergraduate and graduate corporate finance textbooks. Both types of leverage happen in the income statement due to fixed costs. Companies have variable costs and fixed costs. Variable costs vary with revenue such as sales commissions for the sales force, overtime for production, or cost of goods sold, like steel for an automobile manufacturer. Fixed costs are stable and independent of revenue such as salaries and rent. Fixed costs provide operational leverage and interest expense provides financial leverage, as illustrated in Table 10.4.

Table 10.4 Operational and Financial Leverage

	Year 1	Year 2	Growth (%)
Sales	$100.00	$110.00	10.0
Variable Costs	$30.00	$33.00	10.0
Fixed Costs	$40.00	$40.00	0.0
EBIT	$30.00	$37.00	23.3
Interest	$5.00	$5.00	0.0
NBT	$25.00	$32.00	28.0
Taxes	$6.25	$8.00	28.0
Net Income	$18.75	$24.00	28.0

In year one, sales are $100 for a company and variable costs are 30% of sales, or $30. Fixed costs are $40. Subtracting $30 and $40 from $100 leaves $30 earnings before interest and taxes, or EBIT. The $5 of interest is subtracted to get $25 net before taxes, or NBT. An easy tax rate of 25% is used to compute taxes of $6.25. Subtracting taxes from NBT gives $18.75 net income. Let's say from year one to year two sales grow by 10% to $110. Variable costs, at 30% of sales, grow to $33, but fixed costs, being fixed, remain at $40. EBIT has grown by 23.3% to $37. So a 10% growth in sales produced a 23.3% increase in EBIT because of operational leverage. In year two, interest expense remains at $5, so NBT grows to $32, a 28% year to year increase. With the same 25% tax rate, net income increases 28%. A 10% increase in sales produced a 28% increase in net income, so it is normal for income to grow faster than revenue because of operational and financial leverage.

We suspect that the new-age technology companies have a greater percentage of fixed costs and a lower percentage of variable costs than manufacturing firms. The new-age technology companies have salaries that are independent of sales, whereas manufacturing firms buy raw products directly associated with sales. Information technology was the best-performing sector over the eleven-year bull market. So the sweet spots of the bull market benefited from operational leverage and didn't need rapidly growing revenue.

Corporate Debt

Concern began to build in the later years of the bull market that corporations may be carrying excessive debt. As reported in Reuters by Jay Withermuth and Kristen Haunss in an article titled "Yellen Warns of Corporate Distress, Economic Fallout," Janet Yellen, former Federal Reserve chairperson, stated February 27, 2019, "I do think non-financial corporations have run up really, quite a lot of debt. What I would worry about is if the economy encounters a downturn, we could see a good deal of corporate distress . . . . And I think that's something that could make the next recession a deeper recession."

We did our research and wrote the following paper in November 2016, but before getting into it we need to examine Dr. Yellen's track record in securities analysis. Jeff Cox of CNBC.com picked up on it and wrote an article June 2, 2015, titled "Remembering Yell's Awful Biotech Call Last Year." The article began, "As a stock market analyst, Janet Yellen makes a pretty good Federal Reserve Chair. Nearly a year ago, on July 16, 2014, Yellen famously warned of 'substantially stretched' valuations in biotechnology and social media stocks." No wonder he had fun with the article; the S&P 1500 Biotechnology Index gained 42.9% from July 16, 2014, to July 16, 2015. The S&P 1500 gained just 9.4% over that same period. Now back to our research in November 2016 addressing the corporate debt concerns, which offers evidence she may have been equally wrong about corporate debt as she was about biotechnology.

Bond Bubble? Are US Corporations Using Excessive Amounts of Debt?

November 2016

We have heard a lot of chatter lately regarding the corporate bond market. In particular we are hearing concerns about the amount of debt companies are taking on and their ability to honor their obligations. Perhaps these questions are driven by the headlines of corporations issuing debt for either buying back common stock or for acquisitions. Looking at some readily available statistics paints a different picture and may help ease concerns.

Figure 10.2 is the total debt/total assets ratio for the companies in the S&P 500 Index. Essentially it shows the percentage of assets that has been financed through short-term plus long-term debt. Values are as of year-end.

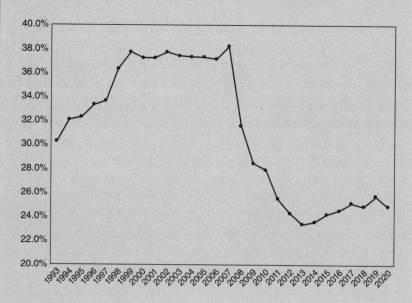

Figure 10.2   S&P 500 Debt/Total Assets

(Naturally we didn't have values beyond 2016 at the time we wrote that paper but have extended the graph for this book.) In the 1990s, the S&P 500 companies financed approximately 30% to 38% of the total assets through debt. For 2000 through 2007 the use of debt was fairly steady in the 37% range. With the recession of 2008–2009, companies deleveraged, reducing the use of debt to financing about 23.4% by 2013. There has been a slight increase in the use of debt since then, but debt use is still far below that of the 1990s and early 2000s.

Figure 10.3 is the debt/equity ratio for the companies in the S&P 500 Index. The 1.50 reading in 1993 indicates companies had $1.50 debt on the books for every $1.00 in equity. The ratio increased in the late 1990s and early 2000s

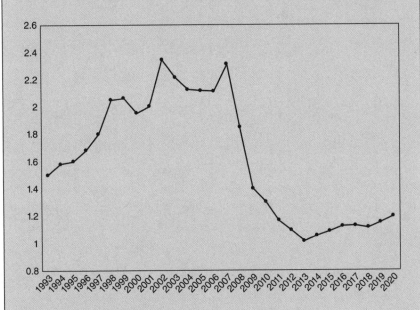

Figure 10.3   S&P 500 Debt/Equity

(continued)

(continued)

to where companies had $2.00 of debt for every $1.00 of equity. Beginning in 2008, we see the similar reduced use of debt as was seen in the debt/total assets chart. There has been a slight increase in debt relative to equity, but debt/equity levels are half of those last decade.

Figure 10.4 is debt/EBITDA (earnings before interest, taxes, depreciation, and amortization). Essentially, it is the cash flow available to cover the obligatory interest payment. As debt use increased in the 1990s and early 2000s, debt rose to $2.30 for every $1.00 of EBITDA. With the reduced use of debt from 2008 through 2013, companies in the S&P 500 Index are functioning with just above $1.00 of debt for every $1.00 of EBITDA.

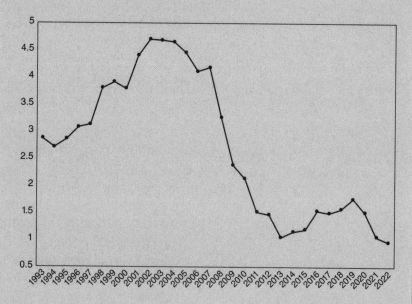

Figure 10.4   Debt/EBITDA

Summary

These three ratios show a big reduction in the use of debt by companies in the S&P 500 Index relative to total assets, equity, and EBTIDA from 2008 through 2013. A slight increase in the use of debt the last three years still leaves these companies far below the debt use levels of the 1990s and early 2000s. This quick analysis would find little support for concerns about the corporate bond market.

There seems to be a belief among investors that corporation managements and boards of directors easily walk away from debt and default. From our perspective, they do not. They have many tactics available, and they go to great lengths to avoid default. We don't know what started the belief in excessive corporate debt. It just seemed to gain a life but was not supported by various debt ratios used by financial analysts. We also know that corporate debt did not cause massive problems (distress) in the next recession, which occurred in 2020.

Inverted Yield Curve

Oh my gosh! The yield curve is inverted! Sell everything and hide under the desk. That was a popular message spring and summer 2019, but obviously ill-advised as the market charged on to record highs February 2020. First, what is an inverted yield curve?

A yield curve is a graph of the yield on government-issued debt instruments with time to maturity on the horizontal axis and yield on the vertical axis. Going left to right, time to maturity increases from three months to six months to one year to two years to five years to ten years and out to twenty years to maturity. Usually the line of those yields slopes upward to the right because long-term interest rates are usually higher than short-term rates. Longer-term bonds have greater price sensitivity to changes in interest rates, so investors usually require a higher yield to compensate for the greater price volatility. But sometimes they don't.

Sometimes the yields from one year out to twenty years are about the same resulting in a "flat" yield curve. Sometimes the yields on the longer-term notes and bonds are less than the yields on the shorter-term paper, resulting in the dreaded inverted yield curve. Economists have noted that recessions have been preceded by inverted yield curves. So when the yield curve went inverted spring and summer 2019, many investors, economists, and money managers predicted a recession and sold stocks.

We do not believe that an inverted yield causes a recession. Rather, whatever causes the recession also causes the yield curve to invert. Here, all arrows point to the Federal Reserve. When the Fed sees a robust, perhaps overheated economy and the potential for increased inflation, it raises its Federal Funds target interest rate. Then, through Open Market Operations, it sells T-Bills to banks, drains reserves, and slows the growth of the money supply. Sometimes it goes too far and causes a recession by accident. Sometimes it may think that the resulting recession is necessary to fight inflation. In either case, it is the raising of the Federal Funds rate, the Open Market Operations, and the resulting slower growth of the money supply that causes the recession. As the Fed is raising short-term interest rates it can also cause the inverted yield curve by moving the short-term end of the yield curve up to and above long-term rates.

What if instead the yield curve inverts because long-term rates come down to short-term rates? Say the Fed is not tightening (not raising short-term rates) but instead, for whatever reason, investors buy long-term bonds and drive long-term rates down to or below short-term rates. It doesn't seem that a recession would necessarily follow that situation. Our theory is that if the inversion is caused by the Fed raising short-term rates, a recession will follow, but if the inversion is caused by the investors buying bonds and driving long-term rates down then there is no recession.

Analysts who monitor the slope of the yields have different measuring tools. Some compare the yield of the 10-year Treasury to the 2-year Treasury. Some compare 5-year maturity to 6-month T-Bills. For our analysis we are using the 10-Year Treasury and the Federal Funds rate because the Federal Funds rate is a specific tool of the Fed. Based on weekly data we found six times when the Federal Funds rate went above the yield on the 10-year Treasury note back to 1980. In Table 10.5 we note the date of first inversion and the Federal Funds rate and the yield on the 10-year Treasury at the time. Just below are those same two rates twenty-six weeks (six months) prior except for 1980. We used fifteen weeks prior because twenty-six weeks before was also an inversion. For the inversions on top a recession did follow. For those on the bottom, there was no subsequent recession and the stock market moved higher.

Table 10.5   Yield Inversions: 10-Year Treasury and Federal Funds

Recession Followed

	Date	Fed Funds (%)	10-Year (%)
Inverted	10/3/1980	12.38	11.40
15 Weeks Before	6/20/1980	8.99	9.49
	Change	3.39	1.91
Inverted	1/13/1989	9.13	9.06
26 Weeks Before	7/15/1988	8.00	9.06
	Change	1.13	0.01
Inverted	4/7/2000	6.00	5.85
15 Weeks Before	10/8/1999	5.00	6.03
	Change	1.00	–0.18
Inverted	6/30/2006	5.30	5.14
26 Weeks Before	12/30/2005	4.25	4.39
	Change	1.05	0.75

No Recession

	Date	Fed Funds (%)	10-Year (%)
Inverted	5/29/1998	5.63	5.55
26 Weeks Before	11/28/1997	5.63	5.87
	Change	0.00	–0.32
Inverted	5/24/2019	2.38	2.32
26 Weeks Before	11/23/2018	2.23	3.04
	Change	0.15	–0.72

Change is the increase or decrease in the rate in the weeks leading up to the inversion. Notice for the times that a recession followed (left), the Federal Funds rate increased by at least one full percentage point in the weeks leading up to the inversion and it increased more than the long-term rate, thereby causing the inversion. On the right, when no recession followed, the Federal Funds rate was either unchanged or barely budged in the weeks leading up to the inversion. The cause in those cases was clearly the drop in the yield on the 10-year Treasury. The data support our theory. If the Fed causes the inversion because of raising short-term rates, a recession is likely. If, instead, the Fed is not tightening and the inversion is caused by investors buying bonds and driving down long-term rates, there is no recession.

Regarding the inversion of May 2019, the Fed had raised the Federal Funds target rate four times in 2018 but held it steady from late December 2018 through the May 2019 inversion, so the Fed was not tightening in the months immediately preceding the inversion. The inversion occurred primarily because of the drop in the yield of the 10-year Treasury note. The Fed dropped the Federal Funds target rate three times in 2019 and the S&P gained 20.8% from that inversion, May 24, 2019, to its peak February 19, 2020. It should be noted that there was a recession in 2020 but it was not caused by the 2019 inversion or tight monetary policy. We shut down the economy on purpose to attempt to contain the spread of COVID-19.

Summary

Although these six situations appear unrelated, they all bothered investors and gave skeptics a reason for selling and missing all or part of the great bull market. Based on the P/E of the S&P 500 Index investors thought stocks were expensive. The fear of deflation sent some investors to the sidelines. Many investors were put off by the corporate buybacks. Some analysts dismissed the earnings growth incorrectly requiring lofty revenue growth. Since 2016, the belief that there was excessive corporate debt was reason for some investors to be cautious, and in 2019, an inverted yield curve proved to be a false alarm. A little simple research, however, defused those concerns. Buying and holding wasn't dull or easy, but it was rewarding.

- P/E is useless in predicting future market returns.
- Deflation isn't necessarily bad.
- Corporate buybacks were correct. Investors were wrong.
- Earnings can grow more than revenue.
- Basic debt ratios show corporations are not overleveraged.
- The cause of an inverted yield matters.

Chapter 11
Active-Passive

Throughout the multiyear bull market it was well documented that mutual funds, on average, did not beat indexes. Promoters of index (passive) investing have spread word of this situation with full force. Significant assets have moved from actively managed funds to passive funds. To understand why assets were moving away from actively managed funds let's analyze the market setting and behavioral finance research regarding active managers. Initially, if we classify stocks by market capitalization and by value-growth characteristics, it can be seen that the first five to ten years of the eleven-year bull market were difficult for active managers due to a setting out of their control.

Market Capitalization

Within the S&P 1500 Index, the S&P 500 Index is composed of the largest 500 companies and the S&P Small-Cap 600 is composed of the smallest 600. Figure 11.1 shows the ratio of the P/E of the S&P Small-Cap 600 divided by the P/E of the S&P 500 monthly from January 1995 through February 2020.

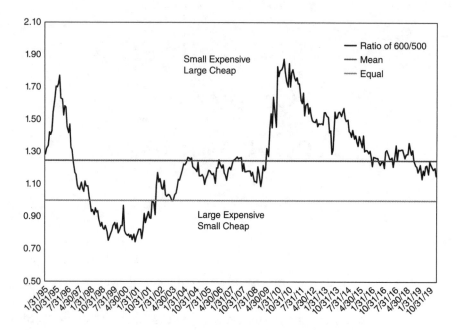

Figure 11.1   Ratio of P/E of Small-Cap 600 to Large-Cap 500

Back to 1995, on average, the P/E on the Small-Cap 600 is greater than the P/E on the (Large-Cap) 500, which makes sense because small companies are growing faster, and investors usually pay a premium for growth potential. The average ratio of the two indexes is 1.25 (top line), meaning, on average, small caps have a P/E that is about 25% above the P/E on large caps. The bottom line is a ratio of 1.00 where they are equal. Any ratio above 1.25 suggests small caps are expensive and large caps are cheap by historic standards. Any reading below 1.25 suggests small caps are cheap and large caps are expensive by historic standards.

Notice how the relationship varies through time. In 1995 and 1996, investors must have loved small caps and took their P/E ratios much higher than normal relative to the 500 Index. Just the opposite in 1999 and 2000, when investors loved large caps so much, they even priced them with P/E ratios greater than that for small caps (below the 1.00 line).

At the beginning of the eleven-year bull market in 2009, small caps were expensive, and large caps were cheap by historic standards, making large caps favored to lead the stock market recovery. Indexes are market capitalization weighted, meaning larger stocks have a bigger weight or influence than small stocks. One way for a manager to try to beat an index is to hold small-cap stocks. For managers, bringing small caps into an active portfolio in an attempt to be different from, and beat, an index wouldn't work when large caps are in favor. Such a setting suggests a difficult environment for active managers and that the best investment tactic was to hug a market capitalization–weighted index and go for the ride.

From the bottom in March 2009 through February 2020, the Small-Cap 600 Index actually did keep up with the (Large-Cap) S&P 500 Index, just not consistently enough nor in the right sectors for managers to boost performance by holding small cap stocks. The Small-Cap 600 beat the S&P 500 only four of the eleven annual periods from 2009 through 2019. From a sector perspective, only four of the eleven sectors in the Small-Cap 600 beat their counterparts in the S&P 500. Most importantly, for all four of the leading sectors for the entire bull market, information technology, consumer discretionary, financials, and industrials, the S&P 500 sector beat its small-cap counterpart. The four small-cap sectors that beat the large caps, like utilities, were lagging sectors that were not going to boost performance by including those small caps. Over the eleven-year bull market, it was not a setting where holding small caps could help beat the market cap–weighted index.

Value–Growth

Within the S&P 500 Index, Standard and Poor's classifies stocks as value or growth. We assume they use metrics such as P/E, price-to-book, and price-to-sales for classifying. Figure 11.2 shows the ratio of the P/E on the growth stocks divided by the P/E ratio of the value stocks from June 1995 through February 2020. Back to 1995,

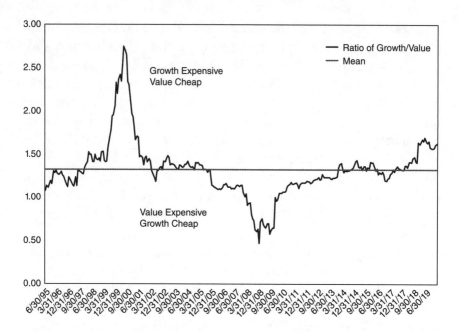

Figure 11.2   Ratio of P/E, S&P 500 Growth/Value

growth stocks have a higher P/E than the value stocks, on average 1.32 times greater (gray line).

Just like with market capitalization, investors' preference for value and growth stocks varies through time. In 1999 and early 2000, investors loved growth so much they priced it much more expensively than normal. At the market bottom of 2009, the love affair totally reversed from the previous extreme, because growth was cheap and value was expensive by historic standards. Combining market capitalization and value-growth metrics, the sweet spot of the market for the early years of the recent bull market was large-cap growth, which is exactly what indexes look like. As the bull market went on, value-growth moved back to neutral by historic standards but for market capitalization, large stayed cheap until late 2015. Because the preferred characteristics were large cap and growth, indexes had a head start over active managers during this bull market. To fully understand why active managers, on average, performed below indexes, we need to look at other factors as well.

Pace

What if the pace of a market advance affects a manager's ability to beat indexes? Maybe some rallies are just too fast for managers to keep up. We looked at the five most recent multiyear bull markets to see if pace and manager performance are related. We divided the total return for the S&P 500 Index from the day of the bottom to the day of the peak by the number of days in the bull market to get percent return per day (pace). In Table 11.1 bull markets are identified by the month and year they began. The first row is the average percent per day return, or daily pace. It can be seen that the three bull markets beginning in August 1982, December 1994, and March 2009 are the three fastest moving, on average, about twice the pace of the other two.

The S&P 500 line is total return for the advance. The S&P 500 and average active manager returns are from a database that tracks managers by their stated strategy (Chapter 12). The strategy database is monthly, so it does not match exactly with the daily data, but it is close. Lag is simply the percent of the index return that the active managers obtained. For example, in the 1982 bull market the average active manager earned 66.7% of what the index delivered. It is clear that in the three fastest-paced bull markets, active managers lagged the most. In the two slowest-paced markets, active managers beat the index in the 2002 bull market and barely lagged in the 1987 market.

Table 11.1 Pace of Bull Markets and Active Management (by Percent)

	8/1982	12/1987	12/1994	10/2002	3/2009
%/Day	0.24	0.11	0.21	0.10	0.19
S&P	280	155	264	108	392
Average	187	147	196	121	267
Lag	67	95	74	112	68

Maybe some bull markets are just too fast for managers. As for reasons, perhaps cash comes in and managers can't or don't get it invested quickly enough. As we saw in Chapter 2, bull markets have big surge days and it is important to participate in them. Maybe cash made funds sluggish during surge days. To confess, we are stuck on finding other reasons pace would affect performance, but it apparently does. This eleven-year bull market was fast enough to give active managers problems.

Changing Market Conditions

Active managers, or stock pickers, have their individual strategies for analyzing and selecting stocks. Most don't change through time. They just keep picking stocks their way. What changes is the market environment, which is a function of a variety of things such as investor sentiment, economic setting, political climate, etc. Recent research is showing that stock picking skill gets rewarded better in some environments than in others. Studies by Larry Gorman, Steven Sapra, and Robert Weigand in "The Role of Cross-Sectional Dispersion in Active Portfolio Management" (2010); Atti Petajisto in "Active Share and Mutual Fund Performance" (2006); and Anna Helen von Reibnitz in "When Opportunity Knocks: Cross-Sectional Return Dispersion and Active Fund Management" (2013) have focused in on three conditions that are ranked by their order of importance:

1. Individual stock cross-sectional standard deviation
2. Individual stock cross-sectional skewness
3. Chicago Board Options Exchange (CBOE) volatility index (VIX)

Let's explain these one at a time before putting them all together. Cross-section standard deviation measures how spread out returns are among stocks. For any month we could compute the average, or mean, return for all the stocks on the New York Stock Exchange (NYSE). We could also compute the standard deviation of all those returns. It would measure how spread out, or dispersed, those returns are around their mean. It turns out that a high standard deviation, or big dispersion, is a good setting for stock pickers. In other words, when there is a big difference between the good stocks and bad stocks, it is easier for a stock picker to get rewarded.

Cross-section skewness refers to how individual stock returns are distributed. Some months the returns for all stocks on the NYSE may be in a perfect normal distribution, often called a bell curve, with an equal number of stocks above and below the mean. Other months return may be skewed, meaning there are an excessive number of stocks with extremely good or bad returns. It turns out that skewness, or an excessive number of stocks with extreme returns, is a good setting for stock pickers, something they can take advantage of.

As for the VIX, the price of a stock option is a function of five variables: the stock price, the exercise price, the risk-free rate of interest, the time to maturity, and the expected volatility of the stock price over the remaining life of the option. We know the first four and can therefore solve the Black-Scholes option pricing equation backwards to determine what investors think volatility is going to be. The CBOE does that and puts out its implied volatility index, known as VIX. Higher levels of VIX is a good setting for stock pickers. Perhaps higher levels of expected volatility result in temporary mispricing that stock pickers can recognize and exploit.

Tom Howard of AthenaInvest has added a fourth influence on the environment for stock picking: small-cap stock premium. As mentioned previously in the chapter, when small cap stocks are performing well, a manager can hold them to look different from, and beat, market capitalization–weighted indexes. Howard has combined the four variables into an equation to compute the Active Equity Opportunity Index, or AEO, which is shown in Figure 11.3 from 1998 through July 2021. Over that period the average is 40. Any reading greater than 40 is a favorable environment for stock pickers. Over this twenty-three year period, 1998 through 2006 and 2008 through 2010 were favorable environments for stock pickers. During the recent eleven-year bull market we were generally in a setting of some combination of low individual stock cross-sectional

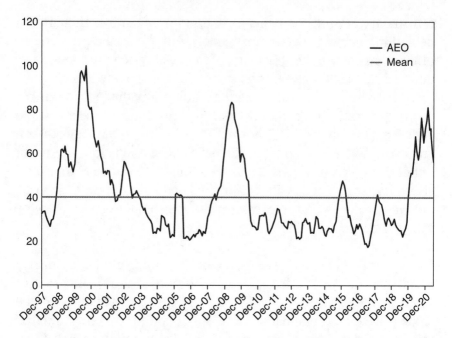

Figure 11.3   Active Equity Opportunity Index, 1/1998–7/2021

standard deviation, low individual stock cross-sectional skewness, low VIX, and no or low small-cap stock premium—a tough setting for stock pickers.

Behavioral Finance

Promoters of passive investing would like to declare that active management is dead but they can't because recent research from behavioral finance gives us a road map to find superior managers. These research results began to appear about 2004 and accelerated concurrent during the eleven-year bull market. They lead us to conclude superior managers do exist. We know how they behave. Therefore, we know how to find them. Generally this research has shown that stock-picking skill does exist and has found behaviors associated with superior performance.

But first a quiz. Do you think superior performance would be associated with which of the following:

a. A manager staying in a style box or
b. A manager selecting favorite stocks from anywhere in the style grid?
a. A fund looking like an index or
b. A manager comfortable with the fund looking different from an index?
a. A fund with a high correlation to an index or
b. A fund with a low correlation to an index?
a. A fund with many stocks or
b. A fund with fewer stocks?

If you answered all *b* you are right. You already know how superior managers behave and do not need to read the rest of this chapter. As for the reasons *b* was correct, let's take them in order.

Russ Wermers, University of Maryland, is a highly skilled researcher. He visited our office a few years back and told how a pension consultant had hired him to do research that would show that style drift was bad. Style drift means selecting stocks that fall in a variety of style boxes rather than selecting stocks from just one box. Wermers had to go to the consultant and deliver bad news. He found that managers who drifted the most performed the best. He concluded constraining a manager to a style box costs about 300 basis points per year.

In 2009, Martijn Cremers and Antti Petajisto, then at Yale, in "How Active Is Your Fund Manager? A New Measure That Predicts Performance," defined what they called "Active Share." It is the willingness of a manager to have a portfolio looking different from an index and can be measured by the percentage of the portfolio that is different from an index. They reported a perfect linear relationship: the greater the Active Share, the greater the performance. They note that "managers with the highest Active Share exhibit some skill and pick portfolios that outperform their benchmarks by 1.51–2.40% per year." They found that funds with a high level of active share and good one-year performance continued to excel.

Two researchers at New York University, Yakov Amihud and Ruslan Goyenko, in "Mutual Fund's R2 as Predictor of Performance," took a similar approach to Cremers and Petajisto and screened mutual funds for two characteristics. They showed that funds with the lowest quintile trailing one-year market R-squared (correlation) to an index and the highest quintile trailing one-year return significantly outperform over the subsequent year. Although Active Share and R-squared are not identical, it is likely that funds with high Active Share will demonstrate a low R-squared. In either case, high Active Share or low R-Squared reveals a manager that does not hug an index. She just picks her favorite stocks.

In the late 1990s when our firm began to market to the public funds institutional market, a plan's pension consultants would say, "I want you to beat the index, but I want you to look like it." That request was based on the notion that tracking error was bad, a cockeyed belief that gained popularity in the 1990s. Now it is clear. Superior managers don't care whether or not they look like an index and their portfolios generally have low correlation to indexes.

A study called "Best Ideas" by Randy Cohen, Christopher Polk, and Bernard Silli, published in 2005 and updated in 2008, yielded startling results with respect to finding superior managers. They ranked holdings in mutual funds by the amount that a stock was overweight or underweight relative to its weighting in the benchmark index. The authors reasoned that the most overweight stocks must be the manager's best ideas and could be ranked by the degree of overweighting. They found that roughly the top thirty stocks generated a risk-adjusted alpha: the best-idea stock beat the second best, the second-best idea beat the third best, and so on. The study concluded, "The U.S. stock market does not appear to be efficiently priced, since even the typical active mutual fund manager is able to identify stocks that outperform by economically and statistically large amounts". Notice the word *typical*. In fact, their statistics suggest that virtually *all* equity managers are superior stock pickers who are able to rank their best ideas. But if this is true, why do studies show that the average mutual fund underperforms? The authors attribute such underperformance to over-diversification and argue that "investors would benefit if managers held more concentrated portfolios". In other words, managers have a limited number of "good ideas." This is powerful confirmation to the simpler study that C. Thomas Howard and Craig T. Callahan published in 2006 in an article titled "The Problematic 'Style' Grid" in the *Journal of Investment Management Consulting* showing that superior returns dropped off at about the fortieth-ranked stock among the four strategies tested. We often tell audiences, "You don't want our seventy-fifth best idea. It's probably not a good one."

We contend that if a manager is rigidly following an investment strategy, its best forty ideas (favorite stocks) don't fall in any one style box, for example, small-cap value. So those best ideas can't be held or the manager would be accused of style drift. To fill out a portfolio and stay in a style box, the manager goes down the list and includes lesser-ranking stocks that do fall in the assigned box. They may be the fiftieth, sixtieth, seventy-fifth, and so on ranked ideas, which as the Cohen article showed are probably not good stocks.

Back to the data driving the move to passive. Why have funds, on average, not beaten indexes during this bull market? Some was due to the large-growth sweet spot. Some was due to the pace of the advance, perhaps simply being too fast for managers to keep up. Also, there are some funds in those averages that are restricted to a style box. There are some funds in those averages that hold 150 to 250 stocks. There are some funds in those averages that either by being so big or by choice hug indexes. In other words, there are funds in those averages exhibiting behaviors that behavioral finance has uncovered to be drags on performance, so they pull down the averages.

Although over the long run, we see behaviors that are drags and behaviors associated with superior performance, they are not always punished or rewarded, respectively. There are some settings, captured in Howard's AEO index, in which the good behaviors just don't get rewarded. They can even be punished in the short run. During the eleven-year bull market, we have had a few of those years.

Passive Investing's Dark Side

In 2016, we wrote a paper taking a different look at the trend toward passive (index) investing. It was called "How Passive Investing Interferes with Our Free Market System" and had a bit of an edge to it.

How Passive Investing Interferes with Our Free Market System

September 2016

This paper will discuss how the stock market helps allocate our society's limited resources. Then it will show how passive investing and index-based ETFs are interfering with our nation's allocation of resources.

Each country has to decide how to allocate its limited resources: land, labor, and capital. Given resources are not unlimited, they are precious and need to be allocated in an efficient manner. An efficient allocation promotes maximum employment and minimal inflation. An inefficient allocation can lead to gluts and unemployment, and/or shortages and inflation. What if society wants housing but excess resources are devoted to making more blue jeans than needed? Home prices skyrocket and workers at blue jean mills get laid off. What if society needs more shoes but resources are used for making dog toys? There would be a shoe shortage but a lot of happy dogs. So how do countries decide how to allocate their limited resources?

In China a group of "really smart people" do it. They decide what will be made and how much of it will be produced. Resources to make bicycles, automobiles, blue jeans, and food are all allocated by a central committee. In the United States, we let the free markets do it, which means the stock market has a critical role. Here's how. Let's say two home-building companies, A and B, go public (issue stock in the primary market) at the same time. They are the same size and issue the same number of shares at $20 per share. Five years later company A has been very successful at building and selling houses. Investors realize the success and its stock is trading at $40 (in the secondary market). Company B has not been successful, so its stock is trading at $10. If both companies want to go back to the primary market and issue more shares to raise capital, the secondary stock market has set the terms. Capital is relatively cheap for A, because it will receive $40 for every new share it issues in the primary market. Capital is expensive for B as it will get only $10 for every new share it issues. The secondary stock market has set the terms for allocating our country's limited resources.

Because of the critical role the stock market plays in allocating our limited resources, and because an efficient allocation of resources is critical to minimize inflation and maximize employment, the stock market has been regulated over the years. It bothers some that the regulations have not taken more of a consumer (investor) protection angle. Instead, to promote efficient allocation of resources, the regulations have been designed to promote participation and stock prices that reflect all public information. For example, the Securities Act of 1933, often referred to as the act of full disclosure, attempted to make sure investors in the primary and secondary markets were getting accurate information. Why? Because in order to protect the integrity of the market, and ensure that all investors have equal access to information to make an informed decision, everyone should know the same information at the same time.

(continued)

(continued)

In short, Congress decided that the rules of the game were to make sure all investors knew all the material facts necessary to make an informed decision. In short, it was necessary to help investors set prices in the primary and secondary markets that would ultimately allocate our country's limited resources in an informed and efficient manner.

Since the passing of the Securities Act of 1933 and the Securities Exchange Act of 1934, all regulation has been based on the belief that maximum participation promotes fair and rational pricing, and maximum participation requires full and equal access to information so important for setting terms for allocating limited resources. The rules against trading on insider information are intended to make sure that the market is not rigged or fair only to those with inside information, because it would prevent or at least discourage everyone else from participating. Lack of participation leads to inefficient pricing.

In short, public equal access to information leads to maximum participation, which in turn leads to efficient markets. Maximum participation leads to fair pricing, which leads to an efficient allocation of society's resources. Diminished participation leads to mispricing and an inefficient allocation of resources.

Professional money managers and do-it-yourself investors do not go to the marketplace every day thinking, "I'm helping society today by setting prices that will ultimately allocate our limited resources." Of course they don't. They are just trying to maximize their returns by investing in the future, but at the same time they are providing a valuable service to society. Index funds and ETFs, which attempt to mirror indexes, do not. In fact, we believe they are hurting society by contributing to an inefficient, wasteful allocation of our limited resources. When investors put money into market capitalization–weighted indexed investments, big companies' share prices are boosted, putting them at an advantage in raising more capital. Even "smart beta" ETFs that tilt toward anomalies or factors, such as momentum, interfere with our allocation of resources. Just because a company's stock has momentum does not mean it should have its stock boosted further by inflows into momentum-based ETFs and therefore give it an advantage in raising capital.

In using the free markets to set the terms for allocating our limited resources we accept the fact that humans are humans, which means they can be wrong, jump on bandwagons, be subject to peer pressure, and chase hot trends to ridiculous levels. We reason that despite these occasional deviations from rational, efficient prices, this system is still better for allocating resources than some other system such as a centralized committee. Index funds and some factor funds magnify and exaggerate the occasional emotional-based deviations, however. Information technology has been on average 17.8% of the S&P 1500 Index based on annual data back to 1995 when the 1500 was introduced. In 2000, at the height of the tech bubble, that sector was 31.5%. Investors putting money into index and momentum-based funds were helping red-hot, money-losing, concept-hopeful technology firms get capital on very favorable terms. Fortunately, we did not have the magnitude of index funds back then that we do now, or in our opinion, technology stocks would have been priced even higher and contributed to an even worse allocation of our resources. When the S&P 1500 Index began in 1995, Financials were 8.5% of

(continued)

(continued)

the broad index but had grown to 20% in 2006 and 18.7% in 2007, at the peak before the financial crisis. Right at the peak, money flowing into index- and momentum-based passive funds were supporting stock prices of financials so they could get capital on very favorable terms to underwrite and resale more and more subprime bad mortgages. The proliferation of index funds and factor ETFs since the last peak sets the potential for an extremely wasteful allocation of our limited resources at the next peak.

As index funds and indexed-based ETFs do not provide superior returns and perform a disservice to society, they should be taxed severely, like a sin tax. One percent of assets would be a sensible starting point for the harm they are causing society. The managers of those funds are shirking their duty. Or, perhaps the size or the amount of indexed investing could be limited, either for the total market or for each mutual fund manager. After reaching a certain level, index funds could not accept new money. In this age of increased emphasis on transparency, passive funds should at least be required to provide disclosure that "investing in this vehicle could cause irreversible harm to society by contributing to increased inflation and unemployment."

The move toward passive investing is threatening our free market system of allocating our limited resources. Unworthy firms may get improved access to capital while worthy firms may find capital prohibitively expensive, potentially resulting in shortages and inflation and/or gluts and increased unemployment. Active management and research rewards and promotes innovation. Passive investing blindly sets prices. Regulations need to return to basics: promote participation in our equity markets, provide full and accurate information, and let pricing in our secondary markets set terms for efficiently allocating our limited resources.

Summary

The large-cap growth leadership of this bull market combined with its relatively fast pace was a difficult setting for active managers. The Active Equity Opportunity Index was below its historic average of 40 indicating an environment unfavorable for stock-picking skills to be effective. In this setting, the behaviors associated with superior performance over the long run, like the freedom of not being locked in a style box, active share, low correlation and fewer holdings, were at times not rewarded and even punished. The volatility events of 2010, 2011, and 2018, as described in Chapter 8, were particularly disruptive to managers with those historically rewarded behaviors.

This bull market presented an interesting cross current. As it advanced, more and more investors switched to passive investing at the same time more and more research appeared confirming the existence of superior managers and identifying their behaviors. Perhaps the next bear market and subsequent bull market will bring these two divergent trends back into line.

- Large-cap growth leadership made it difficult for active managers.
- Perhaps the pace of the advance was too swift.
- Active Equity Opportunity Index confirms it was a difficult setting.
- Passive investing interferes with our allocation of resources.

Chapter 12
Strategies

To investors, all money managers may look alike. They wear business suits. They go on TV and get asked the same questions and generally give the same answers. But they are not all alike. In fact there are some significant differences. If you asked different managers *how* they do what they do, you would immediately see extreme differences as they described their own strategy.

In the early 2000s, we were involved in research that categorized managers of mutual funds by their stated investment strategy. Strategy is how a manager goes about analyzing, buying, and selling stocks. We developed a very expensive and patented algorithm, now the intellectual property of AthenaInvest, which scans the strategy portion of a prospectus looking for elements. Elements are tools a manager uses or standards that must be met for stock selection. Examples would be a P/E ratio, management quality, an economic forecast, or return on equity. We identified ten very different and specialized strategies. Here are the ten investment strategies with brief definitions and descriptions. After introducing those, we will look at strategy performance from 1980 to 2008, before the recent bull market, then 2009 to 2020 during the bull market. It will explain why some managers and investors performed better than others.

Ten Investment Strategies

Here are definitions and description of the ten different investment strategies.

Competitive Position

Fund managers seek companies with traits such as high-quality management, defensible market position, and a track record of innovation. It is easy to see why some managers might implement a competitive position strategy. Intuitively, it would make sense to own companies that have some combination of high-quality management, a record of innovation, and a defensible brand. Notice that this strategy does not attempt to forecast the economy. Analysts simply go out searching for high-quality companies with some type of competitive superiority. Those analysts usually visit companies.

Economic Conditions

Fund managers start with a top-down approach and, using macroeconomic forecasting, work their way down to favored industries and stocks. The economic condition managers begin by forecasting the economy. Then they work their way down to what industries and stocks will do well in the economic setting they expect.

Future Growth

Fund managers search for companies poised to grow rapidly relative to others. Future growth managers seek growth but that can be done in a variety of ways. Some start by focusing on earnings per share growth. Others emphasize revenue or overall company growth. Some managers emphasize sustainable growth and others look for accelerating growth. These companies may have had a moderate rate of growth but are on the springboard to approach a higher level of growth. Future growth managers do not always, nor should they, hold what has been defined to be a growth stock under the style grid.

Market Conditions

Fund managers take into consideration a stock's recent price and volume history relative to the market and similar stocks as well as the overall stock market conditions. The market conditions strategy would include the technical analysts. They begin by looking at things such as stock price chart patterns, relative strength, momentum, or trading volume, among other tools. They may be attracted to a stock by a chart without regard to whatever business the company is in and without any view of the economy.

Opportunity

Employing strategies popular with hedge funds, these managers focus on market imbalances that are driven by events such as earnings surprises, mergers and acquisitions, spin-offs, and companies going private. Opportunity managers are very situational and often event driven. They observe situations or expect events to occur that will affect securities prices. Jim Cramer, on the "Mad Money" TV show, would be an example of an opportunity strategist.

Profitability

Fund managers favor companies with impressive gross, operating, and net profit margins and/or return on equity and return on assets. Profitability is an interesting approach and fairly intuitively appealing. They look for companies that have improving profit margins (income as a percent of sales) or profit margins that are superior to their competitors. They also may be attracted to companies that have improving or above-average return on equity. They do this without caring about the stock's price chart pattern and without any view of the economy.

Quantitative

Fund managers use mathematical and statistical modeling with little or no regard to company or market fundamentals. The computer is programmed to monitor the market and act on situations the programmers believe it can exploit. High-frequency trading would fall into the quantitative category.

Risk

Fund managers look to control risk, with increasing returns as a secondary consideration. When risk managers assess a stock, they are simply looking for low risk. They may use a variety of different variables to determine the risk, such as income statements and balance sheets, volatility of revenues, or even the overall company business model.

Social Considerations

Corporate social responsibility, ecological awareness, or religious tenets are a factor for these fund managers when selecting companies. These managers may look for behaviors or traits or for a lack of these behaviors or traits. In recent years it has been called ESG investing: environmental, social, and governance.

Valuation

Fund managers use financial ratios to determine stock valuations and invest in companies that are underpriced. Valuation managers like to buy companies that are cheap, with many different ways to determine value. Some analysts use simplistic ratios such as price divided by earnings, price divided by book value, or price divided by sales. Others compute intrinsic value perhaps using the dividend discount model or Benjamin Grahams's Central Value Formula. Others may attempt to compute a breakup or liquidation value. Valuation managers may not necessarily hold what, in the style grid, have been called *value stocks*.

Classifying by Strategy

In case you are new to strategies, let's validate them a little and show how different they are from classifying funds by the value-growth, market capitalization characteristics of their holdings (style grid). We have called fund managers and told them what strategy our system put them in. We received 100% agreement in their feedback. They would respond with something like, "You have me. That's what I do." That shouldn't be surprising, however, because they are required to state their strategy in the fund's prospectus, a legally binding document. There is severe punishment for false statements in a prospectus.

These classifications opened up a whole new view of investing and a perspective more insightful and useful than the style grid. In a good classification system, funds in a category should have a high level of commonality with one another. Also in a good classification system, funds in one category should have very low commonality with funds in other categories. The style grid fails those requirements. Returns of funds in any style box, say large-cap growth, have statistically nothing in common with each other, yet they are highly correlated with funds in other boxes. With strategies, it is just the opposite and what should occur with a valid classification system. Returns of funds in any one strategy, say competitive position, experience significant cross correlation with their strategy peers, yet they have much lower correlations with funds in other strategies. That is what you would expect, because managers in a strategy are all selecting stocks in a similar manner and pursuing a strategy very different from the other nine strategies.

As a result, diversifying among strategies can reduce risk because each strategy is doing something very different from the other strategies. Our research shows that diversifying among various style boxes, however, provides no better diversification risk reduction than random selection.

There are a few services that categorize mutual funds into style boxes based on the value-growth and market capitalization characteristics of the stocks held in the fund. We have found all ten strategies in most style boxes, such as large-cap growth. For example, a valuation manager, as determined by the strategy section of its prospectus, would screen stocks by its valuation system, but only hold stocks that meet the large-cap growth restrictions. The same goes for the other nine strategies. They run their strategy but hold the stocks that "fit in the box."

Our research has shown that if a manager rigidly runs a strategy, the thirty or forty highest rates stocks (best ideas) don't fall in one style box. So, the manager faces a choice. Be strategy consistent, hold those best ideas, and get accused of style drift. In that case, the sales department will come storming in and say get back in the box (playpen) or we can't sell the fund to investors. Or the manager can go down the ranking of stocks, find lesser appealing stocks that fit in the style box, and therefore be style consistent, but not strategy consistent.

A manager should be focused in pursuing a strategy because our research shows that the fewer the number of elements that a manager uses, the better the performance. You don't want a manager who forecasts the economy, then looks for value, then considers profitability, and then requires a good-looking price chart, and so on. They don't perform very well. Our research shows that good managers focus on two or three elements and go. As a valuation manager, we have often told audiences, "You don't want us visiting companies. We might get an emotional attachment." We have also told audiences, "You don't want us forecasting the economy. We should just stay focused on value."

Most managers have a primary and a secondary strategy, for example, future growth primary, competitive position secondary. They start with high-growth companies but then as a secondary consideration favor those that are innovative and well managed. Or managers with valuation as the primary strategy and profitability being secondary like stocks on sale but favor those with above-average profit margins. Having a secondary strategy is fine, as long as they are focused on just a few elements. Now let's see how the strategies perform.

Performance

Table 12.1 shows the average monthly returns for the ten strategies from January 1980 through February 2009 (just before the eleven-year bull market began). Over that period future growth and competitive position offered the highest returns.

At the bottom, there is a drop off between the top six and the bottom four. At the very bottom, it appears it was very expensive to attempt to reduce risk during that twenty-nine-year period. As for market conditions, managers using technical analysis, charts, and momentum did not get rewarded relative to other strategies. As for economic conditions, either it is not a good strategy or managers are not good at doing it. We have a guess as to why managers do not get good results using the economic conditions approach. There is always something to worry about, such as inflation, unemployment, consumer and government debt, and so on. Even the typical healthy economic expansion is never perfect in the eyes of critical observers. We guess that economic condition managers, concerned about the imperfect economy, are too cautious and underperform in rising markets. It also turns out that economic condition mangers do well during recessions. It appears they consistently worry and

Table 12.1 Average Monthly Strategy Returns, Jan. 1980–Feb. 2009

Strategy	Return (%)
Future Growth	1.07
Competitive Position	0.94
Opportunity	0.93
S&P 500 Index	0.89
Quantitative	0.85
Valuation	0.84
Profitability	0.84
Average Active Fund	0.83
Market Conditions	0.75
Economic Conditions	0.72
Social Considerations	0.72
Risk	0.67

underperform and then occasionally (and luckily) get rewarded for their persistent concerns when a recession occurs.

Table 12.2 shows the standard deviation of monthly returns, which reflects how much monthly returns deviate from their average. A large standard deviation, for example, would indicate that a strategy has a lot of months with returns well above its average but also many months with returns far below its average. It is often used as a measure of risk. In a twist of irony, risk, a strategy focused primarily on reducing risk, has the highest standard deviation. Future growth, the highest-performing strategy, was second highest in risk. Apparently long-term investors in funds managed with future growth need to fasten their seat belts (and maybe wear a helmet). Valuation was the fifth-best-performing strategy, but lowest in risk, reinforcing the notion that it is difficult to get hurt jumping out a basement window (buying cheap stocks).

Now let's focus in on the unloved bull market. In some ways strategy performance was similar to historic but in other ways very different. Table 12.3 shows strategy performance and reveals and explains the personality of this bull market.

Because these strategy returns reflect only a bull market, they are higher than the historic ones. Similar to historic returns, future

Table 12.2   Standard Deviation of Monthly Returns, Jan. 1980–Feb. 2009

Strategy	Standard Deviation (%)
Risk	6.15
Future Growth	5.29
Market Conditions	4.95
Quantitative	4.62
Profitability	4.50
S&P 500 Index	4.46
Competitive Position	4.43
Average Active Fund	4.39
Social Considerations	4.36
Economic Conditions	4.21
Opportunity	4.07
Valuation	4.01

Table 12.3   Average Monthly Strategy Returns, March 2009–Feb. 2020

Strategy	Return (%)
S&P 500 Index	1.34
Future Growth	1.33
Competitive Position	1.23
Social Considerations	1.20
Profitability	1.18
Quantitative	1.15
Average Active Fund	1.15
Valuation	1.11
Economic Conditions	1.03
Market Conditions	0.96
Opportunity	0.92
Risk	0.80

growth and competitive position were the top two performing strategies. Sector performance may explain some of that edge. We expect their approach to investing pulls them toward information technology and consumer discretionary, the two best-performing sectors during the bull market as shown in Chapter 2. The bottom ones during the recent bull market are similar to historic ones also because economic conditions, market conditions, and risk were three of the bottom four. Why?

- **Economic Conditions.** We can only guess that the imperfect nature of the economic recovery caused the economic conditions managers to be cautious, perhaps holding cash, or defensive, sluggish sectors.
- **Market Conditions.** The rapid industry and sector theme reversals probably caused problems for the market conditions managers using tools such as momentum and moving averages. Also, managers requiring momentum may have missed the initial, and significant, surges of market advances.
- **Risk.** The risk managers were probably invested in defensive, lagging sectors with low betas such as consumer staples, telecommunication services, and utilities.

- **Opportunity.** Opportunity managers are focused on situations and imbalances and apparently missed some of the bull market's broad thrust.

The one interesting position switch from the historic ranking is social considerations, moving up to third best and valuation dropping to fifth worst. We suspect the environmental-social-governance (ESG) approach has a sector bias favoring clean, progressive companies. Perhaps social consideration benefited from the leadership of information technology, consumer discretionary, and even financials. We suspect the ESG selection bias might have been light on energy, the worst-performing sector. However, valuation managers using P/E and price-to-book value may have been sluggish due to being underweighted, information technology, and to a lesser degree, health care. They also may have been hurt by holding energy, but the problem for valuation was more than just a sector tilt. Table 12.4 shows that multiyear bull markets are not when valuation shines, because it only ranked in the top half of strategies once, during the 1982 to 1987 bull market. Otherwise, valuation was bottom half during the other bull markets. It is a real problem for valuation managers that the eleven-year bull market went on so long.

Standard deviation of monthly returns for the multiyear bull market suggests a fairly sensible market. Generally, those who took risk got rewarded. Those who took lesser risk got lesser returns. The three highest-performing strategies had the three highest monthly standard deviations. Perhaps they held high beta stocks. It appears

Table 12.4   Valuation's Rank in Bull Markets

Bull Market	Valuation's Rank
1982–1987	4
1987–1994	6
1994–2000	8
2002–2007	6
2009–2020	6

the key to maximizing returns during the bull market was to hold stocks of rapidly growing companies with innovative managements and accept, or ride through, volatility. The four worst-performing strategies had, in perfect order, the four lowest standard deviations. With market conditions, for example, the use of momentum, moving averages, and stop losses may have dampened volatility but also caused them to miss out on the large surge days mentioned in Chapter 2.

Factors

During this multiyear bull market, a new approach to investing, related to strategies, emerged: factors or factor-based investing. Before relating factors to strategies, let's see where factors came from.

In the 1960s, Eugene Fama published his efficient market hypothesis (EMH). It was stated in three forms: weak form, semi-strong form, and strong form. The weak form stated that current stock prices reflect all information implied in previous stock prices. This means tools such as charts or a momentum measure should be useless for investing. The semi-strong form stated current stock prices reflected all public information. This means that data such as balance sheets, income statements, and P/E ratios will not give an investor an edge. The strong form stated even privileged (inside) information should often be useless for investing. Taken all together it means investors are rational, everybody knows everything, and investors cannot get superior returns. Fama won a Nobel Prize for this theory.

About a decade later articles published in highly regarded journals provided evidence that certain approaches to investing could beat indexes, that is, provide superior returns. One article selected low P/E stocks at the beginning of each year. Another selected low-price-to-book value stocks at the beginning of each year. They both beat the broad market index over their multiyear time periods. Another article reported selecting stocks by momentum. Those resulting returns beat the broad market. Another article selected stocks based on profitability measures such as return on assets or return on equity. That approach beat the broad market.

Defenders of the EMH did what a clever attorney would do, reflect and redirect. At first, using a dismissive phrase, they called them *anomalies,* which is something that deviates from standard, normal, or expected. Then they called them *factors,* a new word for the science of finance. More clever yet, they made *factor* a verb. The efficient market hypothesis held true if you factored out value and factored out momentum and factored out profitability and factored out about a hundred other anomalies. But in the real, un-factored-out, world the EMH didn't hold.

How does this relate to strategies? Factors are elements used by active managers. P/E and price-to-book value are elements used by valuation managers. They know those ratios drive returns some-times. Momentum is an element used by market condition man-agers. They know it works in some settings. Profitability ratios are elements used by profitability managers. They know they work in certain settings.

Marketing executives offer portfolios with a factor tilt. They take an index and increase the weight of stocks scoring high on some factor such as value, momentum, or profitability. But in those cases valuation, market conditions, and profitability managers, respec-tively, are already doing that, without the baggage of all other stocks in the index. Why just stick your toe in the water and get an index with a factor tilt when you can jump in the refreshing pool and hire an active manager using elements to implement a strategy?

Let's tie together Chapter 11, active-passive and manager behav-iors, and Chapter 12, strategies and factors. During this bull market, mutual funds, on average, did not beat indexes. One alternative to active management was to use an index fund. Another alternative that developed was to take an index and tilt it toward stocks scoring high on some factor, such as profitability, value, or momentum, and so on. Just the opposite of factoring them out, as the EMF defenders did to preserve the hypothesis, you factor them in if they can help. Although the name *factor* is relatively new, active managers have been using various ones for decades as tools (elements) for stock analysis and selection under names such as P/E ratio, momentum, and profitability ratios.

There were cross currents during this bull market. As assets were moving toward passive investing and factor-tilted indexes, research was being published that showed that superior managers do exist. Behavioral finance identified manager behaviors that were drags on performance and behaviors associated with superior performance. You want a fund with high active share, low correlation with an index, fewer holdings, and one that is not constrained to a style box. In addition, we know how investment strategies perform over the long run. Combining strategies and behaviors, where was the sweet spot during this multiyear bull market? Future growth and competitive position managers who were comfortable with their portfolios being different from an index and who held concentrated portfolios not constrained to a style box. An investor holding funds from those two strategies with those behaviors would never have considered indexing. Yet they didn't produce every year.

Although future growth was the best-performing strategy over the bull market it wasn't best every year. In 2016, valuation was number one when future growth was the worst-performing strategy, just like it was in the down year of 2008. Competitive position, number two over the bull market was second worst in 2011, a year when market conditions had an unusually good year at number 2. Each year the setting changed, and strategies took their turns getting rewarded.

Behaviors associated with superior performance over the long run were not consistently rewarded during the bull market. The years 2017 and 2018 stand out as particularly harsh. Behaviors historically rewarded, such as high active share and concentrated portfolios, were punished.

Strategies Contributed to "Unloved"?

If managers rigidly stick to their strategy, they will excel in some market and economic settings and lag in others. This look at strategy performance shows what was working during the multiyear bull market and what wasn't. Similar to the time between 1980 and early 2009, future growth managers buying companies with high-growth expectations got rewarded. So did competitive position managers favoring innovative and high-quality management. The bull market was very favorable for social considerations managers selecting companies on ESG ratings. We believe the sector leadership helped those three strategies, but based on the standard deviation of monthly returns they perhaps just followed textbook advice and held high beta stocks in a bull market.

We do not have a survey, but based on our experience market conditions and economic conditions are the two most popular strategies pursued by individual investors. They may use charts and technical analysis and/or they may have a personal outlook for the economy. Professional managers pursuing those strategies did not perform well, so we suspect individual investors didn't either, giving them a reason to sell and get out of the market.

Valuation may also be a popular strategy among individual investors because P/E and price-to-book value ratios are readily available and the notion of buying something on sale is intuitively appealing to many. As valuation didn't get rewarded this last decade, investors using that strategy may have dropped out. As a valuation manager, we were frustrated at times when value would begin to get recognized but then there would be an event and investors would chase or react to the event totally indifferent to value. Relative performance among the ten strategies the last ten years was determined by the economic setting we were in. It changes through time, as do relative strategy performances. Maybe the next bull market will occur in a different setting, but at least for this multiyear bull market, it was likely relative strategy performance helped send investors to the sidelines.

Summary

From a strategy perspective this multiyear bull market was sensible and similar to historic ones in a few ways. Future growth and competitive position did the best. Economic conditions, market conditions, and risk lagged. Valuation, usually not a leader in bull markets, did worse than usual. The strategy performance over such a long bull market may have contributed to investors dropping out. We suspect that economic conditions, market conditions, and valuation, which didn't do well, are three of the most popular strategies among individual investors.

Similar to the move to passive from active investing, there was a move toward factor investing as this bull market developed. We contend active managers with the behaviors described in Chapter 9 using elements will beat factor-tilted indexes.

- There are ten investment strategies.
- We know which strategies work and don't work over the long run.
- During the eleven-year bull market, valuation and social consideration switched.
- We believe managers using a few elements will beat factor-tilted portfolios.
- Some investors dropped out of the bull market because their strategies weren't working.

Chapter 13

Human Behavior

This chapter is going to offer a hypothesis that investors make decisions based on just one variable and that they overestimate the relationship between that variable and the stock market. First, however, let's have one more reminder just how unloved the bull market was.

Short Sellers

Behaviors of short sellers provide a nice summary of how "unloved" the bull market was and how many investors were wrong. To sell short, investors can borrow stock they do not own and sell the shares. If the stock price drops, the investor can buy back the shares (cover) and keep the difference between the selling price and the repurchase price. If the price goes higher, the short seller loses money.

Stock exchanges keep track of shares that have been sold short and not repurchased, called *short interest*. An index computes total short interest on the NYSE, NASDAQ, and AMEX and divides that total by the total float. Float are shares that are outstanding and eligible to be traded. The index reveals what percent of shares outstanding and tradeable have been sold short and not repurchased. It is shown in Figure 13.1 (black) along with the S&P 1500 Index (gray) from December 31, 2008, through November 15, 2019.

At the far left is heavy short selling relative to float in early 2009, before the bottom, at the bottom, and even the first few months of the rally. Apparently, these investors did not believe the rally was sustainable and "for real." But looking back, it was, and those short sellers probably sustained significant losses. Points 1, 2, 3, and 4 show surges in short selling and all reach their peaks at the bottom of market dips. Points 1 and 2 were the severe market drops in 2010 and 2011 due to the European debt crisis rounds one and two. Points 3 and 4 were lesser dips in May 2012 and October 2014. In all four cases, the market drops appeared to be opportunities to sell short for investors with a bearish (negative) mindset. They apparently thought the declines in stock prices would continue, but they

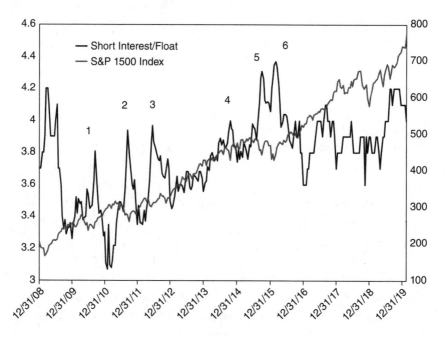

Figure 13.1   Short Interest/Float and S&P 1500 Index, 1/2009–2/2020

didn't. The market turned around, moved higher, and the short positions probably suffered losses.

The actions of short sellers epitomize the bull market. Once it got going, people kept calling for, and predicting, its end. From 2010 through 2015, short sellers increased their activity right along with rising stock prices. Rather than embracing the bull market as it rolled along, they increased their bets against it. Based on the investor sentiment shown previously, plenty of investors thought the market should be going down, but it wasn't. Those bears must have thought prices were irrationally high or that bull markets must have time limitations. Looking back, these two intuitions were wrong.

Short interest, as a percent of float, hit twin peaks in September 2015 and February 2016, again at the bottom of short-term market dips, Points 5 and 6. From there, the S&P 1500 went to successive all-time highs over the next four years. You might think that would be enough to teach the bearish short sellers a lesson and they might throw in the towel, but no. From 2016 to 2018 the short interest/ float index briefly dropped below 3.8% of float a few times, but otherwise remained fairly lofty in the 3.8% to 4% level.

Particularly interesting is the short selling after the low December 24, 2018. In Chapter 9, we described the sharp sell-off of late 2018 as a "volatility event," the third one of this multiyear bull market. As the market marched to new all-time highs in 2019, short selling increased into the market advance. By fall 2019, the short interest/float index was back to levels seen in early 2009. Rather than embracing the bull market in 2019, speculators able to sell short were fighting it. As we know now, the market peaked out February 19, 2020, and the short sellers got bailed out by a virus and pandemic. It is difficult to believe they were selling short in 2019 based on predictions of the consequences of the virus in 2020.

Human Behavior–Economic Forecasting

Why were investors so wrong? Why didn't they recognize a bull market? We have a theory about intuitive-based forecasting.

The stock market is an excellent place for observing human behavior. From that, we have developed a theory about handling cause and effect, but first a little background on economic forecasting. If an economist thinks there is a relationship such that x can predict y, she can run a linear regression. Say she is working with monthly data. She can put in all the observations for x and y each month and an equation will be generated. That equation allows the economist to input a value for x and it will compute what y is expected to be. In Figure 13.2, the straight line represents the linear regression equation. The gray dots represent actual observations. As is normal for economic relationships, the dots are not right on the line. As made up here, the actual observations lie fairly close to the line, which would result in a high-correlation coefficient near the maximum possible of 1.00, meaning a strong relationship between x and y.

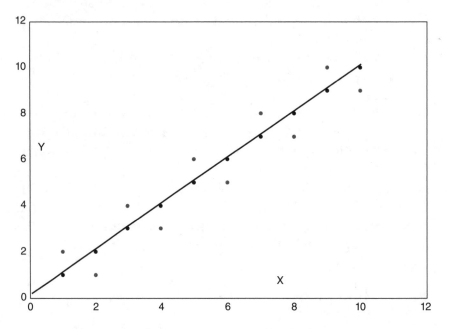

Figure 13.2   Hypothetical Linear Regression, High Correlation

Figure 13.3 shows the same line but with actual observations much further from the line, more like real-world relationships with a lower correlation coefficient. The lower the correlation coefficient, the less accurate the predictions from the equation. Now back to human behavior and our theory. Many investors and portfolio managers do not run econometric models. They rely on intuition. We believe humans overestimate correlation coefficients. They think the relationship between x and y is much stronger than it really is. In other words, if they would run linear regressions, they would find out that x is not as good at predicting y as they thought.

It is normal in economic forecasting to not have single variable models. For example, if an economist is developing a model to forecast inflation, the final model would require perhaps 10 to 20 inputs such as the price of oil, commodity prices in general, wages, capacity utilization, the value of the US dollar, etc. As a result of testing, each input variable would be weighted by its importance.

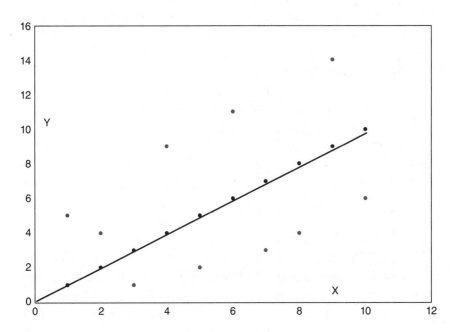

Figure 13.3 Hypothetical Regression, Lower Correlation

The problem is, computer models can handle multiple variable inputs, but human intuition can't. Humans think one variable causes one result, x causes, or predicts, y. They just can't handle p, q, r, s, t, u, v, w, and x all together predict y. It appears using single variable intuitive economic forecasting caused investors to not love the multiyear bull market. For example, they thought lingering unemployment (x) would cause sluggish consumer spending (y), whereas consumer spending is a function of many more variables than just unemployment. They thought above-average growth in the money supply (x) would cause inflation (y), but again, inflation is a function of many variables. In actuality, more things than just x have to line up to move y.

The first two parts to our theory of intuitive forecasting are that the relationship being analyzed is not as strong as believed and the outcome being predicted is a function of a lot more than just one variable. The theory has a third leg. We believe intuitive-based forecasting overestimates the sensitivity of changes in y to changes in x. In statistics it is called the slope of the linear regression equation. Figure 13.4 shows two lines that could have been generated from linear regression of x on y. Line A indicates that small changes in x will result in large changes in y. We think intuitive-based forecasters believe they are dealing with A when an actual statistical test of the relationship would show something more like B. In other words, y is not as sensitive to changes in x as they think.

In Chapter 10, we addressed that during the multiyear bull market there were frequent claims of caution or warnings to get out of stocks based on the P/E ratio of the S&P 500 Index. They were saying that because the P/E was higher than normal, stock prices would either drop or at least could not go higher. As we now know, they were wrong and our three-legged theory explains why. They thought (1) P/E had a much higher correlation coefficient to future prices than it does; (2) future stock prices are a function of a lot more (variables) than just the P/E ratio; and finally, as we showed with our regression in Chapter 10, (3) the slope of the relationship between P/E and future prices is more flat than those prognosticators thought.

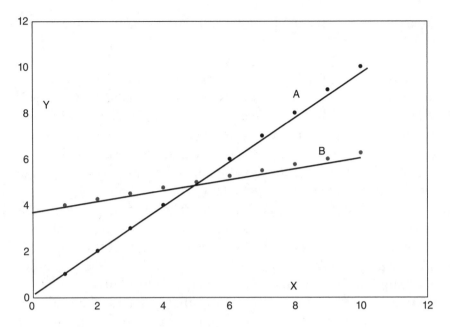

Figure 13.4   Slopes and Sensitivity

In Chapter 3, we showed how a journalist was wrong predicting a problem for bank profits because the yield curve flattened. All three human biases are at work in this example. The correlation between the shape of the yield curve and bank profits is probably not as high as she thought. There are many variables that determine bank profits. And the slope of the relationship between the shape of the yield curve and bank profits is not as steep as she believed.

In Chapter 7, we showed how some observers didn't think unemployment was dropping fast enough. They reasoned it would inhibit consumer spending. From there they reasoned the potential deficient consumer spending would be bad for stocks. Again, these are all three decision-making problems. Unemployment probably has a lower correlation with future consumer spending then they thought. Consumer spending is a function of many more variables than just unemployment. And the slope between unemployment and future consumer spending is probably much flatter than they thought. If we make the jump from unemployment to stock prices the links get even worse.

The end of Chapter 1 referenced three books that for various reasons predicted a bad stock market and proved to be wrong. They all based their predictions on a single variable and overestimated the strength of the relationship between that variable and the economy. Early in the bull market, the first book predicted a decade of slow economic growth and deflation based on deleveraging (debt reduction). The second book, about midway through the eleven-year bull market, predicted the economy would fall off a cliff and warned of a terrible stock market. The third book predicted a severe reversal to the stock market based primarily on global debt. Although all three books could serve as examples of the problem with single-variable forecasting, let's just take the middle one. From innovation to dynamic lifestyles, to changing regulations and taxes, there are probably many more things that influence the economy than just demographics. Then jumping from the economic outlook to the stock market, there are many more variables that influence the stock market than just the economy, such as but not limited to, Federal Reserve monetary policy, fiscal policy, and new product developments.

From inflation to unemployment, from housing starts to consumer spending, people took one variable and overestimated its ability to influence some other variable. We believe their intuitive single-variable forecasting models with three flaws kept them out of the great bull market.

Want to Relive It?

When I was a psychology major at The Ohio State University in the early 1970s, I took a class called "Psychology of Aging." The first day the professor cited a research study. Elderly people were asked if they would want to go back and relive life, in other words, do it all over again. The overwhelming response was "no." To a twenty-one-year-old looking forward to living life, that response was shocking. It just didn't make sense but was worthy of remembering.

This bull market gained 530% in two weeks less than eleven years. Seems fun and easy. Would we want to go back and relive it and do it again? Heck no! It wasn't fun. Just like the old folks in the psychology survey, we have "been there and done that." It was like playing golf with all eighteen holes going in the same direction into a three-club wind. We fought through fears of inflation, deflation, double-dip recession, unemployment, and the rapid theme reversals. Viewing the glass as half full and the day as partly sunny was rewarding, just not always easy. The wall of worry that bull markets always climb just seemed taller this time. Hopefully, reading this book is an easy way for you to relive the bull market and learn how to recognize the next one.

Final Quiz

Who made the most money during this eleven-year bull market?

a. Bearish skeptic
b. Investor looking for alternative investments
c. Someone hiding in CDs
d. Pollyanna who bought and held stocks

The correct answer is D, Pollyanna.

Pollyanna would not have worried about inflation, deflation, double-dip recession, or unemployment. She would have thought the low interest rates were rational and normal. She would have believed in America and believed in the economy, despite its imperfect recovery, and favored cyclical, economically sensitive sectors. She would have believed financials would recover from being the epicenter of the financial crisis and prosper. Pollyanna, on her way to exceptional returns, would have tolerated, accepted, and ignored volatility. At social gatherings or at work, she would not have listened to others talk about the stock market, because they likely would have been bearish and

generally unpleasant to be around. Way to go Pollyanna! Enjoy
the rewards.

- Short sellers didn't believe in the bull market and had bad timing.
- There were problems with single variable forecasting.
- A doesn't cause B as much as you think it does.
- Pollyanna beat the bearish skeptic.

Chapter 14
And Then It Ended with a Crash

One theory states that in Wuhan, Hubei province, China, a case of pneumonia was caused by a novel coronavirus in December 2019. Bats are thought to be regular reservoirs for SARS-CoV-2, but it is unlikely the virus was transmitted directly to humans. It is more likely that there was an intermediate host such as snakes or Malayan pangolins. A pangolin is a scaly, otherwise harmless animal that eats ants. The transmission of the virus from an animal to the human host likely occurred at a live animal market, Hunan Seafood Wholesale Market. At these "wet markets" animals, some exotic, are butchered in a booth adjacent to a booth that might be selling produce. Another theory is that the virus escaped a laboratory in that same province. A third theory is that it originated in a different province. From early March 2020 to early April cases of COVID-19 raced to over a million worldwide, with over 300,000 in the United States. However or wherever it originated, it killed the great bull market.

Stock Market Crash

From the all-time high February 19, 2020, the stock market crashed. In speed and depth, the drop in the market was very similar to the three previous crashes: Octobers of 1929, 1987, and 2008. One difference is that with the previous three, the market was already dropping mildly, then crashed. This time it crashed from an all-time high in just twenty-three trading days. Although those previous crashes included, and gained notoriety from, one or two severe days, they actually unfolded over a few weeks, just like the one in March 2020.

The crash that ended the great bull market had three phases. The first phase, from February 19 to February 28, 2020, was a sharp seven-day drop when investors realized just how contagious the coronavirus was and that it would spread to Europe and the United States. Over these seven trading days, the S&P 1500 Index dropped 12.8%. At the time it resembled the sharp drop of 11.8%, September 17–September 21, 2001, when stock trading resumed a week after the terrorist attacks of September 11, 2001. But unlike 2001, which did not develop into a crash, there was phase two in 2020.

Phase two was ignited in the oil market. Virus containment measures slowed economies in China and other Asian countries, which put downward pressure on the price of oil. At an OPEC+ meeting, Saudi Arabia proposed output reduction to support the price of oil, but Russia refused to go along. Saudi Arabia retaliated by increasing its production, which drove the price of oil even lower. From March 3, 2020, through March 12, 2020, the price per barrel of Brent crude oil dropped 36% while the S&P 1500 Index lost 17.8% over the same period. Investors reasoned that with the price of oil so low there would be energy-related unemployment, defaults, bankruptcies, and earnings problems. During that drop, bankruptcy and default fears can easily be seen in the bond market as corporate credit spreads increased dramatically. Even high-grade bonds took a hit and were not their usual safe hiding place. Moody's AAA bond yield, which is the highest corporate rating, shot up from 2.36% to 4.12% (a 75% increase) in nine trading days. Potential default fears caused a liquidity crisis, a setting of all sellers and no buyers in all qualities of bonds.

Right on top of the oil situation, phase three kicked in. In early March 2020, the administration, Congress, the Federal Reserve, many of us money managers, and the population in general did not realize what extreme containment measures would be necessary, but by mid-March it sunk in. It became apparent that the required containment measures would bring the economy to a halt. On March 12, the PGA cancelled the remainder of the Players Championship amid a rapid sequence of announcements of other closings and cancellations: NBA, MLB, NHL, PGA, LPGA, NCAA, Kentucky Derby, along with restaurants, bars, theaters, non-essential retail, schools, and colleges. Society was shutting down an economy on purpose to stop a disease. During that third phase, stock prices were dropping as economists were slashing their GDP forecasts for second quarter 2020. During the third phase of the crash, from March 13 to the bottom March 23, the S&P 1500 dropped 17.7%.

From the peak February 19 to the low March 23 the S&P 1500 Index lost 34.5% in twenty-three trading days—thanks to a bat, a pangolin, and a virus.

Abnormal Peak

Based on magnitude, a drop of 34% is enough to declare that the great bull market ended a few days short of its eleventh anniversary. Yet that great of a bull market deserved a more dignified ending, a peak with conditions typical of other bull market endings. First would be extremely bullish investor sentiment with a "damn the risk, full speed ahead" approach to investing. Second would be the Federal Reserve tightening to slow the economy and fight inflation. Third would be overpricing in stocks relative to value. None of these conditions existed in February 2020.

Sentiment. The AAII Investor Sentiment Survey (shown in Chapter 1) taken the day of the peak, February 19, 2020, had a ratio of bulls/bears of 141.5%, below its historic average of 146% and below readings seen at previous peaks: October 2007 (212.0%), March 2000 (349.9%), and August 1987 (1100.0%). Typical peak-type optimism was lacking. Instead, there was still a healthy level of skepticism.

Monetary Policy. As for the Federal Reserve, it was not tightening but just the opposite. Its three moves prior to February 2020 had been quarter-point rate reductions in the Federal Funds rate August 1, 2019, September 19, 2019, and October 31, 2019. That easing boosted the Y-O-Y rate of growth of the money supply to 6% to 7%, plenty adequate to support economic growth. Fed easing does not usually end bull markets.

Value. At the peak, the ICON normalized market value/price ratio, an average of about 1,700 domestic stocks, was 1.16 suggesting stocks were priced about 16% below our estimate of fair, or intrinsic, value. Just the opposite of being overpriced at a peak, stocks were, on average, underpriced. In Chapter 1 you saw that this market V/P had been a reliable guide during the eleven-year bull market and it has often been in disagreement with those who thought the P/E on the S&P 500 was too high. There were claims in February that stocks were overpriced based on P/E, but those were the same claims we had seen being wrong for eleven years. They must be discredited because as we showed in Chapter 10, there is no statistical relationship between P/E and stock prices one year later. Stocks didn't drop 34.5% in twenty-three days because they were overpriced. They dropped because society was about to shut down the economy on purpose to attempt to contain a virus, when only weeks before the virus was thought to be unlikely to spread to the United States.

Stunning Visual

From the low of the volatility event December 24, 2018, to the market peak February 19, 2020, the S&P 1500 Index gained 46.18%. As seen in Figure 14.1, it was a fairly steady advance. Then crash!

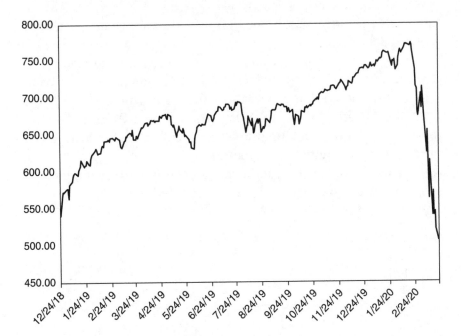

Figure 14.1 S&P 1500 Index 12/24/2018–3/23/2020

The visual shows how stunning the sharp drop was. In twenty-three trading days the index dropped to a level last seen November 11, 2015. The crash wiped out the 75% gain of the final thirty-nine months of the bull market.

We confess to feeling angry at the sudden crash and we wanted our money back, so we turned to a theme often heard in music. Country Western, the blues, and even pop have featured a victim who lost his pickup truck, horse, money, or girlfriend and felt swindled or duped. As this is an investment book, we will stick with money. In various phrasing, they declare, "you may think it's funny, but I lost all my money and I want my money back!"

Off of the March 23 low we started the "I want my money back" tour. We told financial advisors and their investors that we believed we were in a new bull market and to get the money back that the crash took away they only had to do three things: (1) be invested, (2) be patient, and (3) tolerate volatility. We reasoned that doing those three things wouldn't be that difficult and we could get our money back.

In our April 2020 Portfolio Update, which was written a few days after the crash, we stated, "For investing, you have to ask yourself one question. What do you think the world will look like a year from now? If the answer is that the coronavirus will be under control with perhaps even a treatment or vaccine, then we believe it is prudent to own equities at these prices."

The next chapter looks at the market rebound to see if it had the same unloved behaviors as the eleven-year bull market.

Chapter 15

I Want My Money Back

In Chapter 14, Figure 14.1 showed the S&P 1500 chugging its way higher in 2019 and early 2020 and then the swift and severe twenty-three-trading-day crash. As a continuation, Figure 15.1 shows the S&P 1500 Index from its precrash peak of February 19, 2020, through September 10, 2021. The post-crash rally is so spectacular that the crash doesn't look so stunning any more. Two lines are on the graph because the rally changed personality midway through. From March 23, 2020, through September 2, 2020, the market resembled the previous eleven-year bull market in many ways. Then after about a two-month sideways pause, it emerged from an October 30, 2020, low with many different traits and behaviors.

In Chapter 3, we showed how the stock market typically leads the economy by six to nine months and that the economic news is bad at bottoms and good at peaks. We showed how unusual the peak in 2007 was in that the news led the market. Investors who sold on the first bit of bad news got rewarded and potentially avoided the bear market of 2008–2009. They learned a lesson and behavior that proved costly during the great bull market, because selling on bad or disappointing news prohibited the investor from participating in subsequent rallies. Similar to 2007, selling on the first bit of bad news about the virus worked again in February 2020. It is likely that there is a new generation of investors that continued the behavior

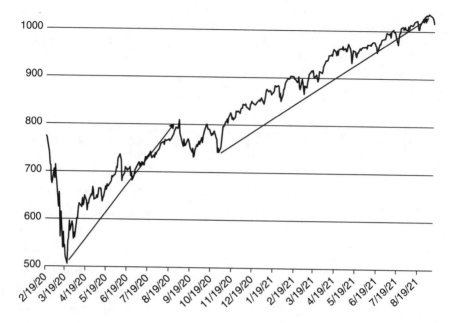

Figure 15.1   S&P 1500 Index

of waiting for good news before buying into the new bull market. As a result, many investors did not participate in the spectacular rally.

Unloved Rebound

Figure 15.2 is the bull/bear ratio weekly for the AAII Investor Sentiment Survey beginning the first week of January 2020. The reading the week of the stock market peak was below the historic average. There were higher readings earlier in the year but still below the one standard deviation line. Notice how fast sentiment deteriorated during the crash. It is normal that it was one standard deviation below its historic average at the bottom, but it is extremely unusual that it didn't improve as the market advanced. The S&P 1500 gained 61.32% from March 23 to the then all-time high September 2, 2020, and sentiment remained extremely bearish. Usually a market advance of that magnitude would attract investors and they would

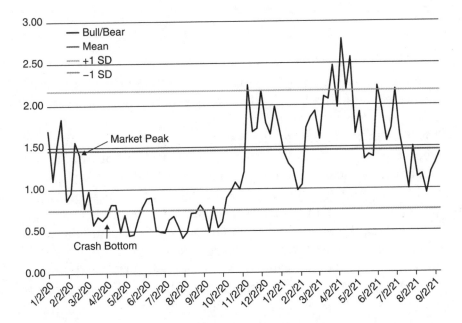

Figure 15.2 AAII Sentiment, Bulls/Bears 1/2/20–9/10/21

turn bullish, but not this time. Investors were scared and dug in. This surely qualifies as at least as "unloved" as the prior eleven-year bull market.

In late October and early November the sentiment changed from bearish to bullish when successful vaccine tests were announced and after the S&P 1500 Index had gained 62%. From that quick jolt of optimism, sentiment slid back down below its historic average. The subsequent increase in bullish sentiment was concurrent with Congress finally passing a fiscal stimulus package. It appears many investors didn't have advanced faith in medical researchers to develop a vaccine or for Congress to pass an obviously necessary stimulus package. As for sentiment to change, they waited for those events to actually happen. By the time the bull/bear ratio got above one standard deviation of its historic average for the second time in late March 2021, the S&P 1500 had gained 80.7% in slightly over one year. As we stated, "rallies don't issue invitations" and "they are usually disguised."

Money Market Fund Assets

Figure 15.3 shows total assets in money market funds weekly from December 31, 2018, through September 9, 2021. During 2019, investors were gradually adding to their money market holdings, perhaps taking profits from the long bull market in equities. In March 2020, however, there were huge flows into the safety of money markets when the stock market was crashing. The subsequent turnaround and gradual descent in money market assets in 2020 is very similar to the sluggish decline of 2009 at the beginning of that bull market, suggesting the initial 2020 rally was at least as unloved as the early 2009 bull market. If investors had correctly realized the stock market was about to go on an impressive eleven-year bull market in 2009 and realized there would be a sharp rally in 2020–2021, money market assets would have rapidly declined both times. But instead, both times investors were slow to take money out of money markets to buy stocks. Worse yet, in 2020 money market assets did not reach

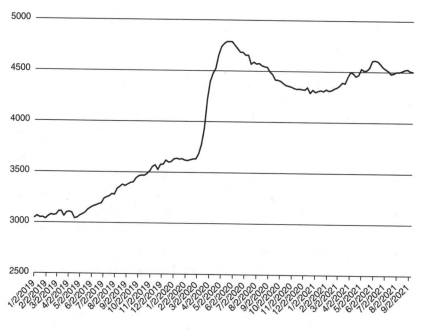

Figure 15.3 Money Market Fund Assets 1/2/2019–9/9/2021

a peak until late May, two months into the rally in equities. In other words, it appears investors were selling into the rally during its first two months and moving to safety rather than buying into stocks. Money market assets the first five months of 2021 resembled 2019, increasing, suggesting investors were selling stocks and moving to safety as the stock market moved higher.

It wasn't just individual investors. Based on interviews on TV and in the print media, many professional money managers were bearish as well and unable to recognize the new bull market. There were many reasons for being bearish and missing out. Some investors wanted to wait to invest until a vaccine had been produced. Other investors doubted a vaccine could be created in a year. Off the March bottom, many observers argued the market would have to retest its low and waited for a "double bottom," which never happened. Some took an economic forecasting approach and only saw a bottomless pit. There were predictions from notable Wall Street economists for unemployment to exceed 20%. There were doubts that the combination of monetary and fiscal stimulus would be effective as we frequently heard a skeptical phrase mentioned previously in the book, "it was like pushing on a string." The most frequently heard reason for a bearish posture was valuation and sounded just like the incorrect claims during the 2009 to 2020 bull market. They claimed the P/E on the market was too high. To address the P/E concerns, here is a paper we distributed in the summer 2020.

Why Claims "The Market Was Expensive" Were Wrong

May 2020

During the rally off the market low, March 23, 2020, many skeptics and doubters have claimed stocks are too expensive and that the rally is irrational. As an example,

(continued)

(continued)

on May 13, 2020, *CNBC Markets* published an article titled "David Tepper Says This Is the Second-most Overvalued Stock Market He Has Ever Seen, behind Only '99," by Yun Li, stating, "Billionaire hedge fund investor David Tepper told CNBC on Wednesday the stock market is one of the most overpriced he's ever seen, only behind 1999. His comments sent stocks to a session low." Mr. Tepper did not mention the basis for his claim but later the article said, "The S&P 500s forward price-earnings ratio based on estimates for the next 12 months has ballooned to above 20, a level not seen since 2002."

The use of the P/E ratio for the S&P 500 Index is a popular tool for gauging the valuation level of the broad market. Unfortunately, those using it have been wrong in 2020 just as they were at the early stages of, and then throughout, the great eleven-year bull market, which began March 2009 and ended February 2020. At the end of February 2009, just before the market bottom of March 9, the P/E on the S&P 500 was 10.95. By the end of November the ratio had soared to 22.08 due to stock prices increasing and earnings dropping. There were claims that stocks were expensive and overpriced, but we know those were wrong as the bull market continued ten-plus more years. Let's see why the P/E ratio is leading them wrong.

The bottom line of Figure 15.4 shows the earnings per share (EPS) for a company growing at a steady 10% per year from a base of $1.00. The top line shows what price would be if investors thought a P/E of 2 was proper all the time. Admittedly, a P/E of 2 is extremely low, but it allows price and earnings to be displayed on the same graph without distortion and doesn't alter the concept.

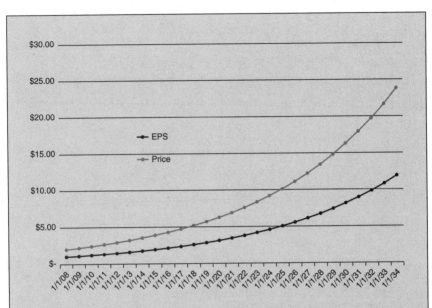

Figure 15.4   EPS with 10% Growth and Stock Price with P/E = 2

What happens if there is a virus pandemic and a self-imposed recession in 2020? Let's say this company's earnings are only $.50 in 2020 and $2.00 in 2021 instead of the $6.28 and $6.90 that they would have been absent the recession. Let's also say the stock price drops sharply at first when investors realized there would be a recession but recovered quickly to where it would have been, again, absent the recession. For most companies this is exactly what happened in 2020: earnings down but stock prices rebounding. This set of events and circumstances is shown in Figure 15.5; note the $.50 and $2.00 EPS in 2020 and 2021.

With earnings of $.50 and a price back to $6.28, the P/E ratio would be 12.6 and would appear astronomical to investors thinking a P/E of 2 is proper. The next year, with earnings recovering a bit to $2.00 and price at $6.90, the P/E

(continued)

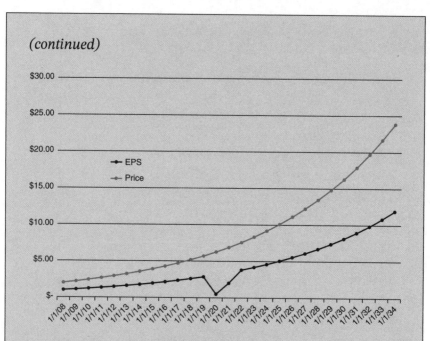

Figure 15.5   EPS and Price with a Recession

would be 3.5, continuing to convey that the stock is expensive. Some users of P/E take current price but divide by EPS one year ahead, as CNBC did in the May 13 article. In this case, 2020 price of $6.28 divided by 2021 earnings of $2.00 gives a "forward" P/E of 3.1, again suggesting the stock is expensive to investors thinking a P/E of 2 is proper.

The use of the simplistic but easy-to-use P/E has many deficiencies. This is just one of them. In financial theory, fair value for a stock or any asset is the present value of future earnings. Given the expectation that earnings will recover and grow at 10% per year, the stock was worth $6.28 in 2020 and the notion that it was expensive because it was priced at 12.6 times earnings was ridiculous.

In 2020, there were some companies on a growth path that was not affected by the virus and recession. At the other end, there were companies whose earnings were severely impacted on by the recession and they do not have good prospects for recovery. For the majority of companies, however, their earnings look like the second graph: down initially and then recovering to their previous potential path. Based on intrinsic value being the present (or discounted) value of their future earnings, the rally of 2020 was very sensible. Investors were pricing in the future, not the present, and stocks were not overpriced.

Sectors

Sector index performance during the first five months of the 2020 rallied, as shown in Table 15.1, and revealed a classic economic recovery anticipation rally. The leaders were economically sensitive and cyclical. The laggards were the so-called recession-proof, defensive sectors. Investors participating in this impressive rally weren't looking at the current economic data; they were looking for improvement six months or so into the future. In other words, they were saying, "Things are going to be better than is currently priced." Investors sitting on the sidelines holding cash didn't have that faith.

Some observers, presumably those who were in cash missing the rally, tried discrediting the advance by claiming the only stocks participating were a handful of "work from home" or "stay at home" stocks. These are companies that actually benefited from the shutdown, such as Amazon.com making home deliveries. The sector returns, however, indicate broad participation. Similar to the 2009 to 2020 bull market, the leadership was composed of high beta (volatility) sectors, whereas the trailing sectors are made up of low

Table 15.1   Sector Returns

3/23/20–9/2/20		10/30/20–9/2/21	
Sector	Return (%)	Sector	Return (%)
Consumer Discretionary	82.9	Energy	78.9
Information Technology	80.4	Financials	61.5
Materials	73.3	Real Estate	48.9
Industrials	65.3	Communication Services	46.8
S&P 1500 Index	61.3	Information Technology	44.6
Communication Services	57.2	Industrials	41.7
Energy	50.9	S&P 1500 Index	41.4
Health Care	48.0	Materials	40.3
Real Estate	45.8	Health Care	36.1
Financials	45.0	Consumer Discretionary	29.4
Consumer Staples	38.7	Consumer Staples	20.8
Utilities	34.6	Utilities	16.2

beta stocks. Similar to the previous eleven-year bull market, investors who accepted and tolerated volatility got rewarded.

As discussed in Chapter 4, it is normal for an economy to first recover and then expand coming out of recession. We suggested during the eleven-year bull market the economy struggled with the expansion phase. The first five months of the 2020 rally priced in recovery and the sector performance resembled that of the eleven-year bull market with information technology and consumer discretionary sectors leading. That is where investors could find growing earnings in a moderate economy. After the September–October pause, however, investors priced in expectations of a robust expansion. Energy and financials moved from the bottom half to being the top two sector performers. Real estate was third and industrials beat the S&P 1500. Investors could easily find impressive expected earnings growth in those leading sectors in the expansionary setting they were anticipating. Information technology fell to fifth and consumer discretionary moved to the bottom half along with defensive, recession-proof sectors. Notice during this second phase investors participating in the leadership had to embrace the economy and have faith in economic expansion. They didn't do that during the eleven-year bull market and hadn't done it since 2005 to early 2007. Embracing the economy and believing in an expansion was new for them.

Strategies

Chapter 12 presented ten investment strategies and showed how they performed during the 2009–2020 bull market relative to their historic performance. During that bull market, future growth and competitive position led as they have historically. Risk, economic conditions, and market conditions lagged, as they have historically. Social consideration and valuation reversed roles with social consideration being among the leaders with valuation lagging. As seen in Table 15.2, the first five months of the rally off the March low of 2020 were quite similar to the previous bull market with future growth, competitive position, and social considerations being the top three. The strategy data come out monthly and do not line up exactly with the daily low and high, but they are close. Similar to during the eleven-year bull market, risk and market conditions lagged

Table 15.2   Strategies

3/31/20–8/31/20		10/31/20–8/31/21	
Strategy	Return (%)	Strategy	Return (%)
Future Growth	46.4	Valuation	44.7
Competitive Position	37.6	Quantitative	41.9
S&P 500 Index	36.5	Competitive Position	41.2
Social Considerations	35.8	Average Active	40.9
Average Active	34.9	Profitability	40.7
Quantitative	34.3	S&P 500 Index	40.1
Economic Conditions	33.3	Social Considerations	39.3
Market Conditions	31.2	Market Conditions	38.8
Valuation	29.7	Future Growth	38.4
Profitability	25.7	Economic Conditions	37.2
Risk	25.2	Opportunity	36.7
Opportunity	22.9	Risk	29.5

and so did valuation again, unlike its historic ranking. Similar to the eleven-year bull market, it was a difficult setting for active managers because the average active manager lagged the S&P 500 Index and only two strategies beat that index.

After the eleven-year bull market, we should be used to this: low investor sentiment suggesting investors do not believe in the rally. The investors who did buy in favored fast-growing (future growth), well-managed, innovative (competitive position) companies. Perhaps they felt they could get their arms around those elements. Just the opposite, it appears investors didn't have enough faith to buy a stock just because it was cheap (valuation). Those investing but trying to minimize risk (risk) missed out as did investors using charts and momentum (market conditions). At the bottom of strategy performance, opportunity managers are very situational and deal to deal, so they missed out on the broad advance. In Chapter 11, we provided a guess that the three most popular strategies among individual investors are valuation, economic conditions, and market conditions. Some may like to buy bargains using readily available valuation data. Some may think they have an informed view of the economy, and some may like to use technical analysis and momentum. But these three strategies weren't working well during the first five months of the 2020 rally, so, with their systems not working, investors may have concluded the rally wasn't sensible or sustainable and sat on the sidelines.

What a complete change after the two-month pause of September and October 2020! From October 31, 2020, through August 31, 2021 (monthly data), valuation took the lead as the best-performing strategy. Profitability jumped into fourth. Future growth dropped to fourth from the bottom. Also note that the average active manager beat the S&P 500 Index as did four of the ten strategies. Did active managers all of a sudden get smarter or work harder? No. A variety of conditions captured in Howard's Active Equity Opportunity (AEO) Index described in Chapter 11 changed. In fact, that index suggested a favorable setting for active managers because there were occasional spikes in the VIX Index, returns among stocks became more dispersed, and skewed and small-cap stocks became the new leaders.

Combining strategies and sectors, the first five months of the 2020 rally resembled the eleven-year bull market. Information technology and consumer discretionary led and were very rewarding to managers employing the future growth, competitive position, and social consideration strategies. It was not a good setting for active managers in general and was as equally "unloved" as the eleven-year bull market. After October 2020, energy and financials led, which was rewarding to managers employing the valuation and profitability strategies. Along with that change, there was a little more bullish sentiment. Perhaps investors can embrace the expansionary theme better than the recovery theme.

Monetary Policy

During the second half of the 2009 to 2020 bull market with low interest rates, many believed the Fed would be helpless if it needed to stimulate the economy. Based on the belief that lowering interest rates is the basis for stimulating the economy, the skeptics argued with rates so low the Fed was out of ammunition. In Chapter 6, we explained that it isn't interest rates that boost the economy but the money supply and that the Fed had three tools to boost the money supply: open market operations, the Discount Window, and lowering reserve requirements. The first two can inject reserves into the banking system, even when interest rates are very low. All three tools enable banks to make more loans, which creates money. Figure 15.6 shows the fifty-two-week rate of growth in the money supply, M1, from October 28, 2016, through February 12, 2021. Initially the Fed was gradually reducing the rate of growth of M1. This bothered investors and finally triggered the volatility event of fall 2018. In 2019, the Fed lowered the Federal Funds rate by injecting reserves three times, which got M1 fifty-two-week rate of growth back up to 6% to 7% by February 2020. In March 2020, as it became apparent the economy would have to be shut down, the Fed kicked into gear. They lowered the Federal Funds rate, injected reserves, and M1 fifty-two-week rate of growth increased to over 40% in a

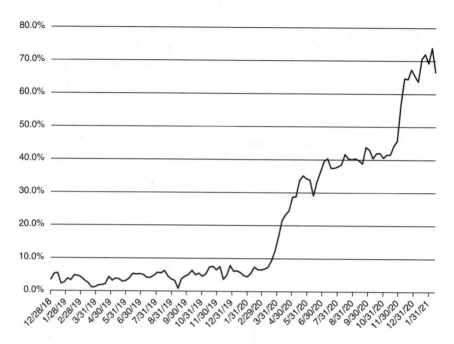

Figure 15.6   Fifty-Two-Week Rate of Change in M1, 12/28/18–2/12/21

few weeks. This certainly shuts down the theory that the Fed is out of ammunition when interest rates are low. They weren't done yet, still having more stimulus capabilities. As Congress seemed politically stalled over a fiscal stimulus package fall 2020, the Fed again injected reserves, banks made loans, and the fifty-two-week rate of growth for M1 increased to 70%. It isn't interest rates that stimulate economic growth, it is M1, and the Fed delivered. We can only guess that investors who thought the Fed would be out of ammunition in a low interest rate setting missed the rally.

Pace

In Chapter 10, it was shown that the faster the pace of a bull market, the more difficult it is for managers to keep up with indexes. From the bottom, March 23, 2020, to the short-term peak, September 2,

2020, the S&P 500 gained 61.38% over 114 trading days. That pace is .54% per day, over double the pace of the three fastest bull markets shown in Chapter 10. As seen in the strategy performance table, the average active manager gained 34.9% and trailed the S&P 500 Index, which was up 36.5%, again based on monthly data. If we had strategy performance data to the day, we suspect the active lag would be worse. The market surged 15.6% the last six trading days of March and caught many managers holding cash and defensive equities. Nevertheless, the first five months of the 2020 rally just add support to the evidence that the faster the pace, the more difficult it is for active managers.

During the second phase and the 211 trading days from October 30, 2020, to the short-term peak September 2, 2021, the S&P 500 Index gained 41.4% for a pace of .20% per day. This slower pace was more favorable for active managers but probably doesn't explain their success as much as the other factors (AEO Index) mentioned in the previous strategies section.

Down Days

In Chapter 2, it was shown that from the bottom to the top of a bull market, the market goes down 44% to 46% of the trading days. The topic was presented to show that the eleven-year bull market was very typical and that bears got incorrect "bearish" confirmation two to two and a half days per week. What about the bull market of 2020? Through its first 134 trading days, the S&P 1500 Index dropped fifty days, or 37.3% of the days. Also in Chapter 2, it was shown that if an investor could just be invested on the best days, it only takes about 2.3% to 5.1% of the total days to get the return of the entire bull market. Through the first 134 trading days of the 2020 rally, we see a different personality than usual. If an investor could have been invested in just the best days, it would have required being invested in 7.5% of the 134 days. With fewer down days and more best days required, the 2020 rally was more of a straight, steady ascent than other bull markets. Investors in cash had to chase it, at higher and higher prices, and short sellers just kept repurchasing (covering) their short positions. Maybe this bull market will go on a few more years. Maybe by then it will look more like typical, choppy bull markets, but in its initial phase, it didn't disguise itself with down days as most bull markets do. It was more of an obvious rally, just unloved.

As for the second phase, the market went down 40.8% of the 211 trading days, closer to the historic average for bull markets and just enough for the skeptical investor on the sidelines to get incorrect confirmation that cash was best.

Economic Surprise

In Chapter 4 there was a graph of the Citi Economic Surprise Index. It was there to show how economists rapidly revised their forecasts during the eleven-year bull market. It suggested some investors might have missed the bull market because they just couldn't get their arms around the economic outlook. Figure 15.7 is an updated version of that same graph from January 3, 2020, through July 23, 2021. The Surprise Index (black) is scaled on the left. The zero line down the middle is when forecasts were accurate with data neither better nor worse than forecast. The S&P 500 Index (gray) is scaled on the right. Leading up to the stock market peak in February 2020, the economic data were generally better than economists had forecast. The market crashed and then the terrible economic data that followed in April and May were much worse than had been forecast. Looking down a "bottomless pit," economists then revised their forecasts downward, way down and too far. From June 2020 through the next twelve months, economic data were better than forecast. They forecasted a horrible economic setting and were wrong. Just to show how far off they were, during the eleven-year bull market the extreme readings for the index when economic data were better than expected were in the 70 to 90 range. In summer 2020 the index hit 250. In terms

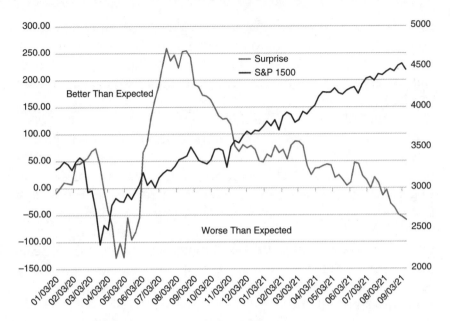

Figure 15.7 Economic Surprise and S&P 500 Index

of the stock market, the crash went too far and priced in a horrible economic setting that didn't happen. Repeating a quote from the book's Introduction, Craig told CNBC TV a few days after the crash. "We do believe a bottom is forming and it seems like all the bad news is priced in." As the subsequent data showed the economy to be bad but not horrible, as previously priced, the stock market rally was very sensible.

Unemployment

Unemployment can serve as an example of economic data that ended up being not as bad as forecast, but first a little background. As discussed in Chapter 7, during the eleven-year bull market many investors didn't participate because they thought unemployment wasn't improving fast enough. Figure 7.2 lined up the peak months of unemployment for the recessions of 1982 and 2009. In both cases unemployment improved at a similar pace. Both times, investors complained it was not improving fast enough, which was apparently irrelevant because in both cases the stock market moved higher.

Figure 15.8 compares unemployment for the recessions of 2009 and 2020. In 2009, there was a gradual buildup, but not in 2020. It was sudden as virus containment measures shut down the economy very rapidly. In 2009, it took twenty-six months from the peak to get unemployment down to 8.4% or better, but in 2020 it took just four months. Both times the stock market moved higher. In 2020, however, rapid improvement in unemployment and the stock market rally were still not enough to get investors off their bearish sentiment. Some investors picked up on the rapidly improving economy and the fact that it was better than had been forecast, but many investors didn't.

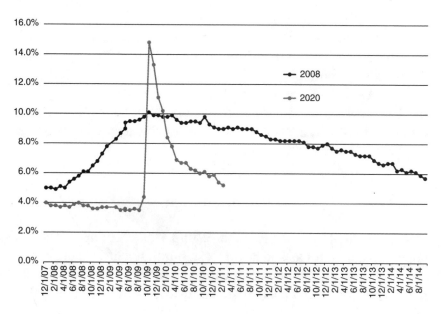

Figure 15.8 Unemployment, 2008 and 2020 Recessions

Value and Sentiment

We have developed a chart in Figure 15.9 to relate value and investor sentiment, which helps explain why the bull market of 2009–2020 and the rally of 2020 were sensible. The outer circle shows investors' view of the economy, ranging from perfect in the upper right to horrible in the upper left. The next circle presents various levels of investor sentiment ranging from greed in the upper right to frightened in the upper left. The second circle from the center is the ICON Market Value/Price (V/P) ratio. As described in Chapter 2,

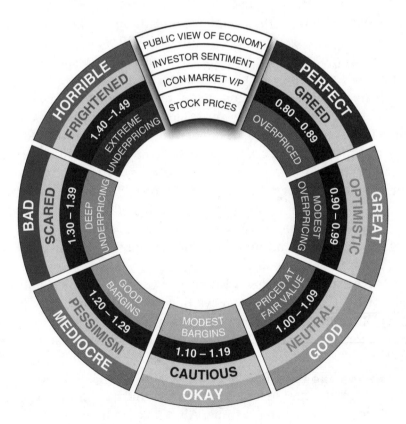

Figure 15.9   Value and Investor Sentiment

ICON estimates intrinsic value for more than 1,700 domestic stocks and divides that value by price. The market V/P is an average V/P of all the stocks in the database. The .8 V/P in the upper right would indicate that an investor buying $1.00 of stocks would be acquiring only 80 cents of value. In the upper left, a V/P of 1.49 would mean an investor is getting $1.49 of value for every $1.00 invested. Finally, the innermost circle just describes the degree stocks are over- or underpriced relative to fair value.

In the upper right, why would investors be willing to invest $1.00 but only get $.80 to $.89 of value in return? Sure stocks are overpriced but investors believe the economy is perfect and greed has taken over. Moving clockwise, if investors think the economy is great, but not perfect, they will be optimistic and still willing to pay more than fair value for stocks. The market V/P of .90 to .99 suggests stocks are modestly overpriced. Continuing clockwise, investors' view of the economy deteriorates. Accordingly, sentiment declines and better and better bargains are available in the stock market.

After the crash of 2020, we were clearly in the upper left section. Similarly, at the beginning of the eleven-year bull market and during the European debt crisis rounds one and two, investors were in the upper left. They apparently saw a horrible or bad economy, were frightened and scared, and gave us an opportunity to buy stocks deeply and extremely underpriced. Most of the time during the eleven-year bull market, however, they saw the economy to be okay to good, displayed sentiment of cautious to neutral, and stocks were priced a bit below fair value.

Maybe investors missed the eleven-year bull market and the rally of 2020 because they were waiting for the economy to be good, great, or perfect, but the economy does not have to be good, great, or perfect for stocks to rally. It just has to be better than what was previously priced in. If investors price stocks for a horrible economy, and it turns out to be just bad, stocks can rally. Then, if investors price in the expectation for a bad economy and it turns out to be just mediocre, the rally can continue. All it takes to ignite a rally is for the economy and the accompanying news to not be as bad as was previously priced in.

Top Ten Reasons

In Chapter 1, we showed how we borrowed from "The David Letterman Late Night Show" early into the eleven-year bull market and tried coaxing investors to get invested. Let's apply that approach to the 2020 rally and look at the top ten reasons investors missed it.

10. I was waiting for a double bottom.
9. There were conflicting calls for the economy to be a V, a U, an L, a K, or even a Swoosh.
8. I forgot the expression, "Don't fight the Fed."
7. I was waiting for everybody to get vaccinated.
6. I was uncertain about the 2020 election.
5. I was busy and in over my head with home schooling.
4. Unemployment was not dropping fast enough.
3. I thought government deficits would cause inflation and higher interest rates.
2. I got scared out (near the bottom) and didn't get back in yet.

And the number one reason I missed the 2020 rally:

1. I heard P/E ratios were too high.

Summary

From the low of March 23, 2020, to September 2, 2021, the S&P 1500 Index gained 109.6%, meaning it more than doubled in seventeen months. Raise your hand if you recognized the opportunity, put all your assets into equities in late March 2020, and then doubled your worth. We expect that if you are raising your hand you may be alone. What would it have taken to be correctly bullish and invested early on and throughout the rally of 2020–2021?

First would be recognizing a market bottom and having the courage to buy in. There is an old saying on Wall Street that it is time to buy stocks when "there is blood in the streets." Late March 2020 certainly qualified. The news was bad and getting worse.

Economists were rapidly and severely revising their forecasts downward. To buy into that bottom, the investor would have had to realize that stocks had fallen too far and priced in a horrible setting that was not going to happen.

Also, various situations needed to be handled to be invested. It was important to recognize that the Fed jolted the money supply and then believed that the jolt would be effective. In terms of a vaccine, it was necessary to realize that there were a lot of really smart, highly motivated people trying to develop a vaccine and that they would succeed. Perhaps most important to be correctly bullish was to ignore the claims that stocks were expensive based on P/E. After recognizing those situations, being invested just required being patient and tolerating volatility.

Here is our commentary from our April 2020 Portfolio Update, written the last week of March.

> As for the stock market, we believe a bottom is forming. Our market value/price (V/P) ratio is at an all-time high and we are seeing many other behaviors and data often seen at bottoms: negative (bearish) investor sentiment, high correlation among sectors, high volatility, decreasing breadth on declines, and, as mentioned, monetary easing and fiscal stimulus. We do not know the exact day of the bottom, but we expect it to be before we see the worst of the news regarding the virus and the economy. This would be consistent with the market's reputation of leading the economy by six to nine months.

Then out of the depths of doom, gloom, and uncertainty the rally unfolded.

- The rebound was very fast.
- As seen by sentiment and money market assets, this rally was as unloved as the previous bull market.
- P/E again proved unrelated to future returns.
- The new bull market had two phases: recovery then expansion.
- Economic data were better than forecast.
- Rallies don't need good news, just better than previously expected.

Chapter 16

Conclusion

C hapter 1 concluded with a graph of the S&P 1500 Index covering the eleven-year bull market. Figure 16.1 is that same graph but extended through September 10, 2021, to now include the 2009 and 2020 bull markets. From the low, March 9, 2009, through September 2, 2021, the index gained 765.42%, meaning $1.00 would have grown to $8.65. In the early stages, $1.00 would have doubled to $2.00. Then the $2.00 would have doubled again to $4.00. Then the $4.00 would have doubled again, plus a little extra. The annualized return was 18.9% over that twelve-year and five-month period.

The ascent is so steep, it makes many of the setbacks and dips along the way appear minor. On the left side, the two European debt crises in 2010 and 2011 don't look as scary as they felt at the time. The sideways volatility of 2015 and early 2016 now appears to be a simple pause. Even the volatility event of late 2018 appears to be just an unpleasant interruption. Based on this figure, it looks like it should have been obvious and easy to invest $1.00 in early March 2009 and turn it into $8.65 in twelve years and five months. It was, as the expression goes, there for the taking. Easy money, but many investors missed it.

In earlier chapters we looked at specific situations that kept some investors out of the market. Some thought inflation was

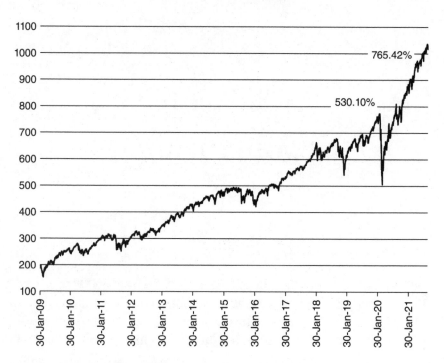

Figure 16.1   S&P 1500 Index

coming back and that interest rates would increase. Some thought unemployment was not dropping fast enough. Some thought stocks were expensive based on a P/E ratio. Some were disappointed with the imperfect nature of the economy, never quite kicking into robust expansion mode. Those were all situational, but what if a primary reason many investors missed the bull market is just due to the quirky way humans reason and evaluate things?

Perceived Uncertainty

In 2003, I did a presentation for financial advisors with Lincoln Investment Planning and their investors. Lincoln called it their South Jersey office, which housed a very good group of advisors. The presentation was making a bullish case for stocks, a correct position as the stock market moved higher the next four years. The audience, however, was worried about the war in Iraq and the questions from investors conveyed that they were uncomfortable with the uncertainty surrounding the war. Then a lady raised her hand and stood up and—*scolded* is too strong of a word—told the audience a thing or two. "I was a little girl when Pearl Harbor was attacked. That was uncertainty. This is nothing." Nobody could disagree with her. That was the greatest audience participation I have ever seen.

There is always uncertainty. We live in a random world with random news. People act like there is uncertainty today but there wasn't uncertainty a decade ago or two decades ago. Sure there was. There was uncertainty in the 1990s, 1980s, 1970s, 1960s, and so on. There was always uncertainty but perhaps some investors thought it was unique to 2009 through 2021.

Gains versus Losses

Psychologists gave us a theory that the pain of losing one dollar is greater than the joy of making a dollar. They tried testing this by using volunteer paid college students, but the results were never convincing because the games they played appeared fabricated. Then they turned to the professional golf tour loaded with a lot of statistics and data. They found that professional golfers were more likely to make a par putt (to avoid bogey) than a birdie putt from similar distances. They reasoned that the bad feelings of getting a bogey and losing a shot to par and the field of players was greater than the perceived good feelings of getting a birdie and gaining a stroke on par. They took this as support for the theory of feelings regarding gains and losses.

Applying that logic to investors and the bull markets, maybe some missed the bull market because they reasoned the benefit of making a dollar wasn't worth the risk of the greater pain of losing a dollar. Where they might have gone wrong was in assigning odds to the two events. Not recognizing that we were in two bull markets, they might have thought the odds of gaining or losing a dollar were equal at 50/50. If instead, they could have looked into the future and envisioned Figure 16.1, they would have realized the odds of losing a dollar were much lower than 50/50. In Chapter 1, it was shown that going back to 1926, the S&P 500 Index produces positive returns 74% of the years. It is fine to be human and feel that the pain of losing is greater than the joy of gaining; investors just need to get the odds of those two outcomes correct.

Type 1, Type 2

The side of Table 16.1 shows that an investor can either buy or not buy a stock or mutual fund. Along the top, that asset can either go up or go down in value. In the upper left, if an investor bought it and it went up, the decision was correct. In the lower right, if the investor did not buy it and it went down, that decision was correct. To borrow from statisticians, there are two types of errors: type 1 and type 2. The lower left box shows the type 1 error because the investor did not buy the asset and it went up in value. A lost opportunity. The upper right shows the type 2 error because the investor bought the asset and it went down in value. Lost money. Which error is worse? You would think it is obvious that losing money is worse than missing an opportunity, but sometimes investor behavior appears differently.

In the late 1990s, with many baby boomers in their forties, investors clearly behaved as though they could not stand missing an opportunity. Neighbors and coworkers were bragging about doubling their money on some dot.com tech stock. Investors wanted to participate and keep up. Also recall from Chapter 1, it was a time

Table 16.1 Types of Errors

	Went Up	Went Down
Bought	Correct	Type 2
Did Not Buy	Type 1	Correct

of high investor confidence as measured by Barron's Confidence Index. So, determined to not make a type 1 error and miss an opportunity, they ultimately ended up making the type 2 error and losing money when the tech bubble burst.

Fast-forward to the 2009 and 2020 bull markets and it is completely opposite. Baby boomers were in or approaching their sixties, and with Barron's Confidence Index very low, investors clearly behaved as though the type 2 error, or losing money, was the worse error and must be avoided. As a result, determined not to make the type 2 error, they made the type 1 error and missed a great opportunity. We propose that if an investor is overly determined to not make one type of error, they will ultimately make the other.

Here is a tangible example of being overly focused on avoiding one type of error but committing the other type. I was raised in northeast Ohio, moved to Colorado in 1979, and brought my beginner-level skiing ability with me. In Colorado, I progressed to where I could handle the intermediate slopes (never did like the darn moguls). I went skiing one day. I skied aggressively all morning, had fun, and didn't fall once. At noon I went back to the car to get my new Canon single lens reflex camera. In a backpack, I took it to the top of the mountain to take some photos. After taking some pictures, I put the camera in the backpack and started to ski down the slopes. Unlike in the morning when I skied aggressively to have fun, my primary objective was to avoid falling and damaging the camera. I fell five times. Investors who invested to make money did a lot better in the two bull markets than investors who invested to not lose money.

Half Empty–Partly Cloudy

We can all see the impressive market gains in Figure 16.1. Living through it, we all saw the same news events and economic data, but we didn't all interpret events and situations the same way. There is a group that sees the glass as half empty and the day as partly cloudy. They earned lower returns than investors who see the glass as half full and the day as partly sunny. The half-empty people, you know who they are, but you can't tell them that they view the glass as half empty. They think they see the world just right. They thought inflation was coming back and interest rates would increase. They thought the low interest rates were phony and fabricated. They thought unemployment wasn't dropping fast enough and that the consumer would quit spending. They analyzed and analyzed and just came to conclusions that bothered them. And the market just kept moving higher. We have concluded, those who can, do. Those who can't, analyze.

When Will It End?

Similar to bull markets and rallies, peaks and the subsequent bear markets don't issue invitations either. They are just as disguised. Here are the behaviors and conditions often seen at market peaks, although all of them don't appear at every peak. The news will be good and expected to get even better. Investor sentiment will be very bullish. In our valuation system, the leading stocks will be over-priced and the underpriced stocks will not be moving or partici-pating in the final advance. We might guess that the promoters of alternatives and volatility reduction products over the last twelve years will turn about and promote all long and even levered long products. The Fed might be tightening and taking the Federal Funds rate above the inflation rate. Investors, however, will be focused on earnings and the healthy economy and will ignore the Fed. Finally, the big clue will be when your "glass is half empty, the day is partly cloudy" friend throws in the towel and gets more equity exposure.

Index

Page numbers followed by *f* and *t* refer to figures and tables, respectively.